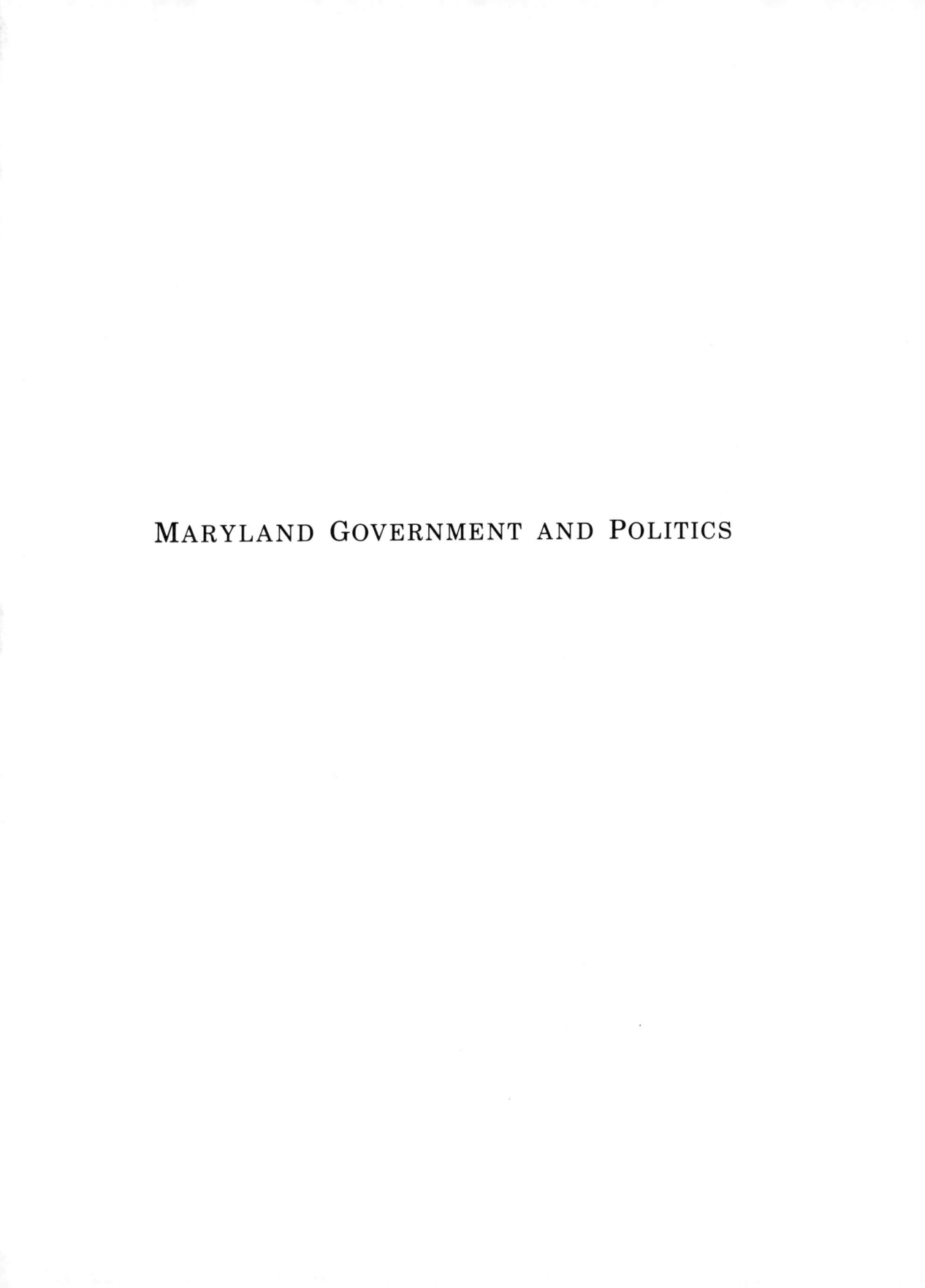

Maryland Government and Politics

MARYLAND
GOVERNMENT AND POLITICS

BY

LASLO V. BOYD
SCHAEFER CENTER FOR PUBLIC POLICY
UNIVERSITY OF BALTIMORE

TIDEWATER PUBLISHERS
CENTREVILLE, MARYLAND

Copyright © 1987 by Tidewater Publishers

All rights reserved. No part of this book may be used or reproduced in any manner whatsoever without written permission except in the case of brief quotations embodied in critical articles and reviews. For information, address Tidewater Publishers, Centreville, Maryland 21617.

Library of Congress Cataloging-in-Publication Data

Boyd, Laslo V.
    Maryland government and politics.

    Bibliography: p.
    Includes index.
    1. Maryland—Politics and government—1951-
I. Title.
JK3816.B69   1987   320.9752   86-40604
ISBN 0-87033-362-3

Manufactured in the United States of America
First edition

Contents

	Preface	6
1.	Introduction	9
2.	The Constitutional System of Maryland	28
3.	The Governor	39
4.	The State Legislature of Maryland	56
5.	The Courts and the Judicial System	78
6.	The Administration of State Government: Bureaucrats and Bureaucracy	97
7.	Local Government in Maryland	114
8.	Baltimore City	137
9.	Politics and Elections	155
10.	Future Prospects	176
	Notes	181
	Suggested Readings	189
	Index	190

Preface

My purpose in writing *Maryland Government and Politics* is to provide students and others interested in state and local government with a basic source of information about Maryland. While there are a number of useful materials available (and they are cited throughout this book), there is no current volume which takes a comprehensive view of state and local government in Maryland. The intent of this book is to fill that gap. In addition, my hope is that those who read it become more interested in, and knowledgeable about, the public policy issues that face state and local government, and that they become more involved in the political process as well.

While I bear ultimate responsibility for this book, there are many people who have assisted me and who have contributed to the ideas and information that are presented here. I have had the benefit of numerous discussions with both students and faculty members at the University of Baltimore. I want to particularly thank my colleagues in the Department of Government and Public Administration, Richard Swaim and Larry Thomas, for their suggestions and comments.

I've also had the opportunity to learn much from people directly involved in government and politics in Maryland. While this list is a long one, I want to mention specifically two names. When I moved to Baltimore in early 1972 to work for him, William Donald Schaefer had just become mayor. As this book nears its publication date, he is about to finish 15 years as mayor and to become governor of the State of Maryland. The opportunity to observe his tenure in office has been a learning experience of great value.

The other person to whom I owe a special debt is Mark K. Joseph. I have worked with him as the city's Development Coordinator, as the President of the City Board of School Commissioners, and as an actively involved private citizen. Throughout this association, he has not only provided me with opportunities to get involved in the processes of government but shared as well his own knowledge and perspective.

In the preparation of this manuscript, I received financial support from the Research, Grants and Lectures Committee of the Yale Gordon College of Liberal Arts. I also received invaluable help from my graduate research assistants, Ann Daukzsewicz, Diane Kaslow and, especially, Gayle Fink. Diane Aull, Portia McCormack, and Sandra Witherspoon were able to decipher my writing and turn it into a typed form, which I recognize was not an easy task.

I am happy to acknowledge the kind permission extended by Greg Stiverson of the State Archives to reproduce various pages from the *Maryland Manual* [pages 25, 58, 59, 60, 72, 105, 109, 165, and 168] and by James H. Norris, Jr., State Court Administrator, to reproduce charts and tables from the *1984-85 Annual Report of the Maryland Judiciary* [pages 80, 81, 82, 84, 85, 86, 87, 88, and 89].

My last thanks go to my wife, Patti, and my daughters, Erica and Carrie. Although they were not involved directly in the preparation of this book, it is really written for them.

Baltimore, Maryland
November 1986

Chapter 1

INTRODUCTION

State and local governments affect our lives in important ways every day. Our counties are responsible for the public schools our children attend, the state maintains many of the highways we travel on, and both state and local agencies deliver such essential services as law enforcement and trash removal. Although the activities of the federal government receive the most attention in the news media, it is actually the workings of our state and local governments that have the most direct impact on us.

Many citizens know relatively little about the organization and operations of our state and local governments. Public opinion polls reveal that we are more likely to be able to identify national officials than local ones. Voter turnout is less for local than for national elections. Citizens often view state and local government as entangled in a maze of incomprehensible regulations and procedures.

However, if government is to be responsive to public needs, there must be an informed and attentive citizenry. While some people are politically active and concerned, there are many others who are uninterested or unwilling to take the time and effort to be informed or involved.

This book describes the structure and functioning of state and local government in Maryland. It offers a basic resource for all readers who need information on the subject. The broader goal is to stimulate reader interest in state and local government and to provide a sound foundation for participation in the electoral process and decision making at this level.

PORTRAIT OF THE STATE

A statistical profile of Maryland reveals a number of distinct characteristics as well as a significant diversity within the state. Maryland can be seen as both a whole and as a number of different parts.

The state's total population, according to the 1980 census, is 4,216,975, ranking it twentieth in the United States. At the time of the first national census in 1790, Maryland's population of 319,728 ranked it sixth, also slightly above the middle. Therefore, relatively speaking, Maryland's rank has not changed very much over the years. The total land area of 9,837 square miles makes the state one of the smallest, forty-second in the rank of the fifty. The combination of a large population and small size results in the state being the sixth highest in population density in the country, over 428 people per square mile.

This density figure conceals a variation within the state ranging from about 40 persons per square mile in Garrett County to more than 9,700 persons per square mile in Baltimore City. Differences in total population by political subdivision are similarly wide; Baltimore City has 768,938 compared to Kent County's 16,577. (See Table 1-1.) These differences are but one example of the diversity within the state. Others will be discussed throughout this book.

While Maryland's total population has been growing—7.5 percent between the 1970 and 1980 censuses—there have been significant shifts within the state. Baltimore, the only large city in Maryland, has been losing residents, while suburban areas have been growing steadily. (These changes are also shown in Table 1-1.) According to one national study:

> Maryland has a clear suburban majority—the only state in the country that can make that claim . . . it's the suburbs that are coming to define the state politically, through the sheer force of numbers.[1]

Specific characteristics of the population also show significant variation. The state's median age of just over 30 mirrors the national average, but within Maryland, the range extends from St. Mary's County's 26.1—St. Mary's also has the highest birth rate in the state—to Talbot County's 36.8.

Approximately 400,000 Marylanders are age 65 or older, which constitutes just less than 10 percent of the state's total population. That figure is slightly less than the national average of 11.3 percent, but this figure varies from 5.1 percent in Howard County to 17.5 percent in Talbot County. Baltimore City, with more than 100,000 residents over 65, has by far the largest number of senior citizens of any subdivision in the state.

The under-eighteen population totals 1,167,530, or 27.7 percent of the overall state population. The proportions in this instance differ from 17 percent in Charles County to 33 percent in St. Mary's, with Baltimore City again having the largest total, over 200,000.

The over-sixty-five and under-eighteen segments of the population are sometimes referred to as dependent. While that characterization does not accurately describe everyone in these groups, these two groups, as a whole, are the least likely to be employed or economically self-sufficient, and, therefore, will not make a significant contribution to the tax base of the community. Most of the under-eighteen group is in school. The over-sixty-five population is most likely to be retired from full-time emloyment, but there is great variation within this group in terms of both resources and needs.

Another population characteristic, race, has received considerable attention in recent years. The issue of racial relations has been a sensitive one in many communities in the United States.[2] In Maryland, blacks now comprise approximately twenty-three percent of the population, roughly double the national figure. Forty-five percent of Maryland's blacks live in Baltimore City, making up fifty-five percent of the city's total population. By comparison, neighboring Baltimore County has less than nine percent blacks and Garrett County less than one percent. These population differences form the basis for differing attitudes on race relations across the state as well as affect the extent to which racial concerns are a factor in local politics.

The citizens of Maryland are among the most highly educated in the nation. Over twenty percent of the population have college degrees, a figure that ranks the state fourth in the United States. Over sixty-seven percent have high school diplomas. There are over one million Marylanders in school each year as well. Table 1-3 shows a breakdown of this last statistic, by elementary, secondary, and higher education, and by public and private schools. Public expenditures for education total close to $2 billion each year, making education the largest category of state and local government spending.

Maryland is a relatively wealthy state. Measured by per capita personal income, for example, Maryland ranks ninth in the country with

Table 1-1. POPULATION OF MARYLAND BY RACE AND POLITICAL SUBDIVISION, 1980 AND 1970

Subdivision	1980 Census Total	White	Black	Other
MARYLAND	4,216,941	3,158,838	958,150	99,987
Allegany	80,548	78,942	1,299	307
Anne Arundel	370,775	321,203	42,860	6,712
Baltimore City	786,741	345,113	431,151	10,511
Baltimore	655,615	590,283	53,955	11,377
Calvert	34,638	26,733	7,689	216
Caroline	23,143	19,138	3,915	90
Carroll	96,356	92,818	2,840	698
Cecil	60,430	56,825	3,204	401
Charles	72,751	56,787	14,736	1,228
Dorchester	30,623	21,394	9,086	143
Frederick	114,792	107,511	6,344	937
Garrett	26,498	26,340	61	97
Harford	145,930	131,347	12,167	2,416
Howard	118,572	101,354	13,899	3,319
Kent	16,695	12,895	3,683	117
Montgomery	579,053	493,485	50,756	32,812
Prince George's	665,071	391,427	247,860	25,784
Queen Anne's	25,508	21,278	4,080	150
St. Mary's	59,895	49,357	9,540	998
Somerset	19,188	12,433	6,639	116
Talbot	25,604	20,082	5,449	73
Washington	113,086	107,555	4,752	779
Wicomico	64,540	49,945	14,085	510
Worcester	30,889	22,593	8,100	196

Source: Maryland Department of Economic and Community Development, *Maryland Statistical Abstract 1986-87.*

an average of $13,000. This figure, as with previous ones, conceals the considerable disparity in both wealth and income across the state. Table 1-4 compares the twenty-four subdivisions of the state by per capita personal income, family income distribution, and percentage of the population living below the poverty level. The existence of these differences raises numerous public policy questions for both the individuals involved and for the governmental jurisdictions in which they live.

Subdivision	1970 Census Total	White	Black	Other
MARYLAND	3,923,897	3,193,021	701,341	28,037
Allegany	84,044	82,704	1,198	142
Anne Arundel	298,042	262,268	33,288	1,983
Baltimore City	905,787	479,837	420,210	5,712
Baltimore	620,409	599,027	19,555	2,495
Calvert	20,682	12,956	7,690	36
Caroline	19,781	15,736	4,025	20
Carroll	69,006	66,127	2,736	143
Cecil	53,291	50,194	2,794	303
Charles	47,678	33,820	13,422	436
Dorchester	29,405	20,271	9,086	48
Frederick	84,927	78,800	5,931	196
Garrett	21,476	21,338	112	26
Harford	115,378	105,267	9,419	692
Howard	62,394	56,573	5,016	322
Kent	16,146	12,158	3,963	25
Montgomery	522,809	493,934	21,551	7,324
Prince George's	661,719	561,441	91,843	7,283
Queen Anne's	18,422	13,824	4,583	15
St. Mary's	47,388	38,522	8,404	462
Somerset	18,924	11,800	7,113	11
Talbot	23,682	17,578	6,084	20
Washington	103,829	99,813	3,789	227
Wicomico	54,236	42,636	11,512	88
Worcester	24,442	16,397	8,017	28

One final set of statistics is worth adding to this profile of Maryland. The nature of the state's economy is changing, as reflected in Table 1-5, from manufacturing to service industries. This change is, in large measure, part of a national trend.[3] Within Maryland, the process of adjustment and response to that trend has affected different parts of the state in different ways. Howard County, largely undeveloped in 1970, has been the site of enormous economic growth as new businesses have moved to that area. By contrast, the loss of a large amount of manufacturing in Baltimore City has led to efforts to find replacement businesses.

Table 1-2. 1980 MARYLAND POPULATION UNDER 18 AND OVER 65

Subdivision	Total Population	Population Under 18	Percent of Population Under 18	Population Over 65	Percent of Population Over 65
MARYLAND	4,216,975	1,167,530	27.69	395,609	9.38
Allegany	80,548	20,136	25.00	12,389	15.38
Anne Arundel	327,915	105,986	32.32	25,085	7.65
Baltimore City	786,775	211,943	26.94	100,575	12.78
Baltimore	655,615	147,574	22.50	169,939	25.92
Calvert	34,638	11,532	33.29	2,871	8.29
Caroline	23,143	6,603	28.53	3,170	13.70
Carroll	96,356	28,385	29.46	8,991	9.33
Cecil	60,392	19,093	31.62	5,553	9.19
Charles	72,751	12,501	17.18	4,005	5.15
Dorchester	30,623	7,860	25.67	4,766	15.56
Frederick	114,792	34,270	29.85	10,211	8.89
Garrett	26,498	8,238	31.09	3,160	11.93
Harford	146,730	39,196	26.71	9,371	6.39
Howard	118,572	36,491	30.78	6,081	5.13
Kent	12,895	2,936	22.76	2,034	15.77
Montgomery	579,053	154,311	26.65	50,905	8.79
Prince George's	665,071	194,624	29.26	36,508	5.49
Queen Anne's	25,508	6,969	27.32	3,083	12.09
St. Mary's	59,895	19,995	33.38	4,015	6.70
Somerset	12,433	2,876	23.13	2,194	17.65
Talbot	25,654	6,016	23.45	4,469	17.42
Washington	113,086	29,761	26.32	13,501	11.94
Wicomico	64,540	17,026	26.38	7,755	12.01
Worcester	30,889	7,881	25.51	4,257	13.78

Source: Maryland Department of Economic and Community Development, *Maryland Statistical Abstract 1986-87.*

For individuals, periods of unemployment and the need to develop new skills have resulted from the changes in the economy. These phenomena are not limited to Baltimore City, but can also be seen in other traditional manufacturing areas such as Hagerstown, Cumberland, and Salisbury.

Changing economic conditions have required adjustment and response. Government has gotten more involved in trying to affect the economy and in dealing with the impact of it. This has led to economic competition at every level of government from the international to the

Table 1-3. ENROLLMENT IN PUBLIC AND PRIVATE SCHOOLS, ALL LEVELS, MARYLAND, FALL 1984

Type of School	1984
Total All Levels	1,044,934
Total Prekindergarten through High School	811,024
Public	673,840
Kindergarten and Prekindergarten	54,474
Elementary (1-8)	283,036
Secondary	336,330
Private	137,184
Kindergarten and Prekindergarten	33,675
Elementary (1-8)	64,418
Secondary	39,091
Total Four Year Colleges and Universities (includes graduate enrollment)	132,974
Public	102,584
Private	30,390
Total Two Year Colleges	100,936
Public	99,575
Private	1,361

Source: Maryland Department of Economic and Community Development, *Maryland Statistical Abstract 1986-87.*

local. The interrelationship between economic conditions and governmental activity is reflected in such data as employment and unemployment figures, the cost of programs for the poor and needy, and government tax revenues.

The numbers presented in this section are intended to help give a picture of Maryland and of the residents of the state. Statistics in any book are always somewhat out of date and do not deal with all subjects or issues. Moreover, no attempt has been made here to examine the figures on Maryland's population in any great detail. This data should, however, provide a broad overview of the principal characteristics of the state and of major distinctions that are contained within it.

MARYLAND AS A MICROCOSM

Maryland has been called "America in miniature."[4] It makes no difference whether or not the state *is* really a microcosm of the United

Table 1-4. INCOME AND POVERTY IN MARYLAND

	Per Capita Personal Income (Dollars) 1983	1978	Percent Change	Median Income 1979	Families Below Poverty Level: 1979 Number	Percent
MARYLAND	13,047	8,397	55.4	23,112	82,012	7.5
Allegany	9,102	6,141	48.2	16,927	1,994	9.0
Anne Arundel	12,696	8,142	55.9	24,771	4,862	5.0
Baltimore City	10,057	6,605	52.3	15,721	35,751	18.9
Baltimore	14,099	9,348	50.8	24,413	7,337	4.1
Calvert	11,813	7,573	56.0	23,831	680	7.7
Caroline	8,932	6,263	42.6	17,105	638	10.1
Carroll	11,832	7,744	52.8	23,340	1,017	4.0
Cecil	10,027	6,770	48.1	20,144	1,083	6.9
Charles	11,318	7,254	56.0	25,747	1,135	6.2
Dorchester	9,433	6,354	48.5	16,699	884	10.7
Frederick	11,563	7,646	51.2	22,639	1,496	4.9
Garrett	7,287	5,037	44.7	14,959	902	12.7
Harford	12,029	8,035	49.7	23,565	2,403	6.2
Howard	15,622	10,039	55.6	30,328	919	2.9
Kent	10,120	6,604	53.2	16,347	460	10.2
Montgomery	19,738	12,193	61.9	33,702	4,661	3.0
Prince George's	12,939	8,187	58.0	25,525	8,138	4.9
Queen Anne's	10,585	7,065	49.8	19,514	530	7.4
St. Mary's	10,120	6,199	63.3	20,573	1,229	8.3
Somerset	7,957	5,329	49.3	14,602	568	11.0
Talbot	13,780	8,763	57.3	19,733	514	7.1
Washington	9,832	6,918	42.1	19,333	2,440	8.0
Wicomico	9,571	6,703	42.8	18,446	1,555	9.0
Worcester	10,619	7,046	50.7	16,620	816	9.7

Source: Maryland Department of Economic and Community Development, *Maryland Statistical Abstract 1986-87*.

States. The great diversity and variation contained within the boundaries of Maryland do, however, make a difference. Moreover, there have been significant social, economic, and political changes that have occurred in recent years that have required responses and adaptations on the part of the citizens of Maryland. Government, both at the state and the local levels, has been the principal institution through which those adjustments have been made.

Table 1-5. NONAGRICULTURAL EMPLOYMENT IN MARYLAND, 1984, 1979, AND 1974

	Annual Average Employment (1,000 Jobs)			Percent of Total			Employment Percent Change	
	1984	1979	1974	1984	1979	1974	1984-79	1979-74
Employment	1,081.7	1,691.3	1,493.6	100.0	100.0	100.0	6.5	13.2
Manufacturing	218.1	246.9	254.5	12.1	14.6	17.0	−11.7	− 3.0
Durable goods	116.4	138.6	140.8	6.5	8.2	9.4	−16.0	− 1.6
Nondurable goods	101.7	108.3	113.7	5.6	6.4	7.6	− 6.1	− 4.8
Nonmanufacturing	1,583.6	1,444.4	1,239.1	87.9	85.4	83.0	9.6	16.6
Mining	1.6	2.0	1.8	0.1	0.1	0.1	−20.0	11.1
Contract construction	114.5	107.4	105.4	6.4	6.4	7.1	6.6	1.9
Transportation, excluding railroad	43.2	42.1	38.4	2.4	2.5	2.6	2.6	9.6
Railroad transportation	7.3	9.7	10.5	0.4	0.6	0.7	−24.7	− 7.6
Public utilities and communications	39.6	34.2	32.0	2.2	2.0	2.1	15.8	6.9
Wholesale trade	99.8	86.9	72.0	5.5	5.1	4.8	14.8	20.7
Retail Trade	349.4	312.5	277.3	19.4	18.5	18.6	11.8	12.7
Finance, insurance, and real estate	103.8	89.8	80.0	5.8	5.3	5.4	15.6	12.3
Services	440.5	341.1	272.6	24.5	20.2	18.3	29.1	25.1
Federal government	133.0	131.6	132.7	7.4	7.8	8.9	1.1	− 0.8
State and local government	250.9	287.1	216.4	13.9	17.0	14.5	−12.6	32.7

Source: Maryland Department of Economic and Community Development, *Maryland Statistical Abstract 1986-87*.
Note: Figures may not add to total due to rounding.

Harborplace in Baltimore City

The idea that Maryland is a microcosm of the United States springs from the significant diversity within the state. Although the total geographical area of Maryland is only 9,837 square miles of land, making the state forty-second in size, there are a number of clear, distinguishable parts of the state. One can even look at these parts in different ways.

A pictorial overview might highlight the beaches of Ocean City, the mountains of Western Maryland, the rolling farmland of Central Maryland, and the urban core areas of Baltimore City. An analysis based upon major media markets would focus on Baltimore and the Washington D.C. area, with everything else left over. City, suburban, and rural areas could constitute another breakdown.

A more comprehensive approach is taken in a recent historical study of Maryland which concludes that there are four distinct cultures within the State: Baltimore City; the suburban areas; Western Maryland; and the Eastern Shore and Southern Maryland. George Callcott, in *Maryland and America 1940 to 1980*, comes to the conclusion that each of

Division of Tourist Development, Maryland Dept. of Economic & Community Development

Bicyclists on Ocean City's boardwalk

these areas has a distinct identity, the combination of which composes the character of the state.[5]

There are a few particular characteristics that have also drawn attention. One is the central importance of a body of water, the Chesapeake Bay, to the entire state. The Bay touches much of the state, is a key element in its economy, and represents a distinctive and unique feature of Maryland as compared to other states.[6]

Maryland's geographical location also gives rise to several observations. Whether the state is northern or southern is a continuing discussion, although of less significance today than in the past. Being part of the great urban northeast megalopolis, which extends from Boston to Washington, D.C., certainly helps to define the state. Having the nation's capital as a neighbor also has influenced the character of Maryland.

What is significant about these characteristics of the state? For one thing, there are some real and identifiable differences in characteristics within Maryland, which, in turn, lead to different needs with respect to government. Two aspects illustrate this point. Densely popu-

Allegany County Tourism & Public Relations   Photo: Richard Springer

Allegany County's rolling hills

lated areas require more services such as public safety than do rural areas. Sections with a strong and growing economic base will be less dependent on state resources than those areas whose economies are stagnant and which have a large proportion of the population not self-sufficient.

On another level, the existence of sections of the state with a clear sense of self-identification will limit the extent to which there are single, overall approaches to state issues. The idea of local control is one with strong support in the United States generally, with Maryland following the general pattern. While there have been many factors contributing to greater centralization of government activities in this country, local identification is one which resists that trend. Many key public policy questions end up focusing on the relative roles of the state government and of local jurisdictions.

INTRODUCTION 21

Traditional row houses in Baltimore City

In addition, politics within the state reflects local differences. Coalitions form in the legislature in response to differing perceptions of local needs. Candidates for statewide office are often seen as from a particular area and campaign to persuade other sections of the state of their suitability for office. Shifts in population, which in turn alter the size of legislative delegations, affect the ability of different sections to pursue their interests with respect to statewide issues. Table 1-6 shows

M. E. Warren

The twin-span Chesapeake Bay Bridge

the changes in percentage of the state's total population for each of the four areas identified by Callcott. For example, Baltimore City has declined from a majority status in 1920 to having one-fifth of the population in 1980. At the same time, the suburbs, which did not exist in 1920, constituted over 60 percent of the state's population as of 1980.

Maryland's relationship to the rest of the nation is affected by the state's characteristics as well. For example, its relatively small population makes Maryland politically less significant than large states such as California and New York. The state's northeast location and changing economic base result in a perspective on certain national issues that differs from, for example, Arizona's or Florida's.

Some of these factors are more permanent than others. The Chesapeake Bay is going to remain important in the future. The significance of specific businesses and industries to the state's economy may change

Table 1-6. THE FOUR CULTURES OF MARYLAND

Area	\multicolumn{3}{c}{Percentage of State Population}
	1920	1940	1980
Baltimore City	51	47	19
Eastern Shore and Southern Maryland (including Anne Arundel and Prince George's counties to 1939; Charles County to 1979)	22	16	11
Western Maryland (including Baltimore and Montgomery counties to 1939; Carroll and Howard counties to 1959; Harford County to 1969)	27	18	10
Suburbs (including Anne Arundel, Baltimore, Montgomery, and Prince George's counties in 1940; Carroll and Howard counties in 1960; Harford County in 1970; and Charles County in 1980)	0	19	61

Source: United States Department of Commerce, Bureau of the Census. Cited in George H. Calcott, *Maryland and America 1940–1980*.

over time, as they have in the past. The nature of change and the balance between continuity and change are of central importance in any community.

GOVERNMENT IN MARYLAND

Among the many functions of government in our society are the resolution of differences among citizens and the development of techniques for coping with potentially adverse changes in our environment. While government is not the only institution involved in these processes, we have assigned significant formal authority to government and have expected it to play a key role in exercising that authority.[7]

Representative government in Maryland dates back to 1635, over three hundred and fifty years ago. The first legislative body met in St. Mary's City a year after Maryland received its colonial charter from King Charles I. Maryland was one of the original thirteen colonies that declared their independence from Britain in 1776 to form the new United States of America and was the seventh state to ratify the United States Constitution, on April 28, 1788.

Citizens of Maryland played key roles in the early development of the United States and the state was the location of many important

Laurel Racecourse

Horseracing is a billion-dollar industry in Maryland. Shown is the track at Laurel.

events. The first president of the United States, under the Articles of Confederation in 1781, was John Hanson of Maryland. The key meeting which led to the Constitutional Convention in Philadelphia in 1787 was held in Annapolis the prior year. Francis Scott Key wrote "The Star-Spangled Banner" in 1814 after witnessing the shelling of Fort McHenry during the War of 1812 with Britain. A Marylander, Roger Taney, played a critical role in the early development of the United States Supreme Court, serving as Chief Justice from 1836 to 1864.

Maryland was a focal point, both geographically and politically, during the Civil War. Key battles were fought in Maryland, and there were sharp divisions among the state's citizens about the war. This period of change included two new state constitutions, in 1864 and 1867.

The state, since that period, has played a less central role in national developments although the major trends of industrialization and urbanization were both evident in Maryland. The growth of the federal government, particularly after the Great Depression and World

INTRODUCTION 25

REVERSE

OBVERSE

The Great Seal of Maryland

War II, has had a major impact on Maryland and on the citizens of the state as well. Changing views about the appropriate role of government in our society have also had a widespread and profound effect.

The precise nature of that role and of our expectations about it have continued to change and to be a matter of public discussion and debate. Certainly our confidence in government fluctuates. Moreover, we may have different views about the various levels of government—federal, state and local.

In contrast to centralized governmental systems, the American system of federalism allows state and local governments to make important decisions and to undertake significant activities.[8] State and local governments are the ones that deliver services directly to the public and with which we are most likely to have contact.

We count on our governments (national, state, and local) for a wide range of services, some of which we receive individually and some of which are distributed on a collective basis. The former category includes programs as diverse as unemployment compensation and agricultural subsidies while highway construction and environmental clean-up programs are good illustrations of the latter. Government's concerns range from the life-and-death issues of national defense and law enforcement, at one extreme, to such mundane matters as filling pot holes and collecting trash, on the other. Polls suggest that we are usually more aware of and concerned about the level of performance in taking care of the pot holes and the trash.

Over a number of years, regulations issued by government have come to influence large parts of our lives and activities. Some of those regulations affect the way in which the economy operates, such as restrictions on monopolies, while others attempt to protect citizens from dangers, such as health regulations for restaurants and food-handling operations. At times, there is public criticism of excessive government regulations, but there are also frequent calls for new regulations as a remedy for an existing problem.

For those who perceive that neither governmental services nor regulations have a direct effect on their lives—and the above remarks should demonstrate that such a perception is clearly erroneous—there is still the matter of government taxation. Our national, state, and local governments collected over $671 billion in taxes in 1982, an average of $2,963 from each of us.

Yet, for many of us, government and politics are subjects either to ignore or to make jokes about. Public opinion polls show with great regularity that neither our knowledge about nor our confidence in government is very high. For example, an alarmingly high number of citizens cannot name their elected representatives. At the same time, however, there are others of us, admittedly fewer, who are deeply involved in and concerned about government and politics. These individuals may have government jobs, may run for elected office, may try to influence the actions of government, and may have strong feelings about public issues.

There is actually a third group in addition to these two. Many citizens pay little attention to government most of the time, but may become interested and active when a particular issue or action affects them directly. As often as not, the concern will be to get government action to remedy a problem. On occasion, the source of the problem may be perceived as government itself, in which case the remedy will be seen as the cessation of government activity.

Despite being built on the theory of representation, the workings of our system of government are characterized by a great deal of inattentiveness by citizens and by a great deal of inconsistency of opinion. For example, citizens may favor expanding particular government services, but may be opposed to raising the revenues to pay for those services.

The premise of this book is that government and public policy will benefit from a well-informed citizenry. Citing the mistakes of some governments and the shortcomings of some public officials, cynics conclude that the public gets the kind of government it deserves by its neglect. The ancient Greeks believed that awareness of and involvement in public life were essential ingredients of citizenship. The more positive perspective of this latter view is the approach followed here.

Chapter 2

THE CONSTITUTIONAL SYSTEM OF MARYLAND

A basic characteristic of all systems of government is the existence of a set of fundamental rules that outline and define the powers of government and the ways in which those powers are to be exercised. We refer to these fundamental rules as a constitution. Constitutions can take many different forms, written as the United States Constitution is, unwritten as in the British version, or a combination of the two. Constitutions also vary in the amount of detail and specificity they include, ranging from broad outlines to very definite rules and regulations. A constitution, as the fundamental governing document of a political system, is intended to be permanent. While constitutions may be amended or reinterpreted, the creation of a new constitution usually reflects the change to a new political system.

The U. S. Constitution, written in 1787 and adopted in 1789, is most often thought of as referring exclusively to the federal government. In fact, the Constitution sets out rules and restrictions that apply as well to state and local governments; it also helps establish the relationship among the different levels of government. The Founding Fathers, who met in Philadelphia in 1787, were most concerned with what the balance of power between the national government and the states should be. The system that they established, which has come to be called federalism, specified certain activities as the exclusive domain of the national government, left others, referred to as "reserved powers," to the states, and expected some functions to be performed by both national and state governments (see Table 2-1). The exact balance has shifted constantly since 1787 and continues to do so today.

Table 2-1. THE AMERICAN FEDERAL SYSTEM DIVISION OF POWERS BETWEEN THE NATIONAL GOVERNMENT AND THE STATE GOVERNMENTS

	Powers Granted by the U. S. Constitution	Powers Denied by the U. S. Constitution
National Government	**Delegated** To coin money To conduct foreign relations To regulate interstate commerce To levy and collect taxes To declare war To raise and support military forces To establish post offices To establish courts inferior to the Supreme Court To admit new states **Implied** "To make all laws which shall be necessary and proper for carrying into execution the fore-going powers, and all other powers vested by this Constitution in the Government of the United States, or in any Department or Officer thereof." (Article 1, Section 8:18)	To tax articles exported from any state To violate the Bill of Rights To change state boundaries
National and State Governments	**Concurrent** To levy and collect taxes To borrow money To make and enforce laws To establish courts To provide for the general welfare To charter banks and corporations	To grant titles of nobility To permit slavery To deny citizens the right to vote
State Governments	**Reserved to the States** To regulate intrastate commerce To conduct elections To provide for public health, safety, and morals To establish local governments To ratify amendments to the federal constitution	To tax imports or exports To coin money To enter into treaties To impair obligations of contracts To abridge the privileges or immunities of citizens or deny due process and equal protection of laws

Observers of federalism in action have, from time to time, attached a label to the term in an attempt to characterize it more fully.[1] "Dual federalism" refers to the decentralized system in which the division between federal and state activities was very clear and in which states and local governments were responsible for almost all the public services provided directly to citizens. As late as 1930, there were only fifteen federal grants to states, totaling less than two percent of state revenues.[2]

The period from 1933, with the election of Franklin Roosevelt, to 1960 has been called "cooperative federalism." The federal government became much more active in areas that had traditionally been state functions. The number of programs grew to 117, with a value of nearly $7 billion. Through grants, regulations, and subsidies to business, the federal system became much more centralized, and the role of states diminished in importance.

The trend toward centralization went even further between 1960 and 1980 (see Table 2-2). The number of federal programs increased to more than 500 and the federal grant dollar amount went up to $91.5 billion. New programs previously not undertaken by any level of government were part of this movement, as was expansion of regulation mandated by the federal government. Examples include the growth of social service programs as well as the increase in social and environmental regulation.

The expanding role of the federal government has at times been accompanied by observations that states no longer have a significant role to play, that they are obsolete.[3] While the federal constitution insures that states will continue to exist, it does not guarantee them any particular role. There is no question that the balance between the federal and state governments has shifted significantly, but there has also been adaptation and adjustment at the state level.

One of the strengths of federalism is that it provides the opportunity for innovation and experimentation by individual states. In addition, there has been a great deal of revision and reorganization of the powers and structure of state governments. There have been ten new state constitutions since 1960, significant amendments to others, and a general revival of thinking about the performance of state government.[4]

There has also been political activity. The "new federalism" advocated by Ronald Reagan after he became president in 1981 stressed the shifting of a number of functions from the federal to the state level.[5] While there is unlikely to be a return to a decentralized system in the

Table 2-2. FEDERAL GRANTS TO STATE AND LOCAL GOVERNMENTS, 1960-1980

Year	Amount (Billions of Dollars)
1960	7.0
1965	10.9
1970	24.0
1975	49.8
1976	59.1
1977	68.4
1978	77.9
1979	82.9
1980	91.5

Source: United States Department of Commerce, Bureau of the Census, *Statistical Abstract of the United States.* Washington, D. C., 1984.

United States, there is ample evidence that state and local governments will continue to play a significant role in the future. The flexibility of the U. S. Constitution has allowed these shifts in balance while also maintaining limits on the functions of government.

The Constitution of the State of Maryland operates within the broad framework of the U. S. Constitution. State constitutions may not contradict provisions of the U. S. Constitution. Rather, they elaborate on the powers and functions that are left to the states by the U. S. Constitution.

History of the Maryland Constitution

Maryland has adopted four different constitutions in its history: in 1776, 1851, 1864, and 1867. The 1867 document, which consists of a declaration of rights, the operational sections of the constitution, and the amendments, is in effect today.

The longevity of the Maryland Constitution is somewhat misleading. The document, in contrast to the U. S. Constitution, is lengthy, very detailed, and has been amended frequently. Maryland's constitution has over 40,000 words and nearly 200 amendments, compared to the approximately 4,200 words and 26 amendments in the U. S. Constitution. While the broad structure of government remains as it was developed in 1867, significant changes have been incorporated.

The process of change is worth noting. The Maryland Constitution, in Article XIV, allows the General Assembly, by three-fifths vote of

An older view of Maryland

both houses, to propose amendments, which are voted on at the next General Election. The combination of very specific provisions in the original 1867 constitution and of the changing conditions and needs since then has resulted in the amendment process being used nearly two hundred times since 1867. Moreover, amendments, which apply to only a particular county or to Baltimore City, require a majority vote in that jurisdiction as well as statewide.

Changes in constitutional meaning come by other means as well, the most important being interpretation by courts. Both the federal courts, particularly the U. S. Supreme Court, and state courts have reevaluated key provisions of the Maryland Constitution over the years. In addition, changing interpretations of the U. S. Constitution have affected the workings of the Maryland Constitution.

A pivotal example is the issue of reapportionment.[6] Prior to 1962, courts were unwilling to become involved in the drawing of legislative district boundaries. In that year, the U. S. Supreme Court, in *Baker* v. *Carr*, 369 U. S. 186 (1962), ruled that the federal constitutional guarantee of equal protection of the law applied to legislative apportionment. A series of decisions which followed, including *Maryland Committee* v. *Tawes*, 377 U. S. 656 (1964), established the one-man, one-vote principle and fundamentally altered political relationships in many states. In Maryland, the composition of both the General Assembly and of local councils was shifted as a result.

The Maryland Constitution has another provision for change. The General Assembly may call for a constitutional convention to consider revisions. In addition, every twenty years, Maryland voters are automatically given the opportunity to decide if they want to set up a constitutional convention. A convention was in fact established by the legislature in 1967. A new constitution was proposed, but was rejected decisively by the voters in 1968.[7] Many of the proposed changes have been added as amendments to the current constitution since then. Maryland voters will have another chance to vote on calling for a constitutional convention in 1990.

Provisions of the Maryland Constitution

The Maryland Constitution begins with a Declaration of Rights consisting of forty-six articles. This Declaration of Rights section is a combination of specific rights that parallel the Bill of Rights of the United States Constitution—for example, freedom of press and speech

> **Article XIV.** Amendments to the Constitution
>
> SEC. 2. It shall be the duty of the General Assembly to provide by Law for taking, at the general election to be held in the year nineteen hundred and seventy, and every twenty years thereafter, the sense of the People in regard to calling a Convention for altering this Constitution; and if a majority of voters at such election or elections shall vote for a Convention, the General Assembly, at its next session, shall provide by law for the assembling of such convention, and for the election of Delegates thereto. Each County, and Legislative District of the City of Baltimore, shall have in such Convention a number of Delegates equal to its representation in both Houses at the time at which the Convention is called. But any Constitution, or change, or amendment of the existing Constitution, which may be adopted by such convention, shall be submitted to the voters of this State, and shall have no effect unless the same shall have been adopted by a majority of voters voting thereon.

are included in Article 40—and general statements of governmental principles, such as Article 34's observation that rotation of office in the Executive Department "is one of the best securities of permanent freedom." The section also includes specific operating rules of government, such as Article 11's provision that the legislature will meet in Annapolis.

The specific enumeration of individual rights in the Maryland Constitution has been important because provisions of the U. S. Bill of Rights have not always applied with equal force to the states.[8] Moreover, the Maryland Constitution has had the opportunity to go beyond the federal constitution, as in the inclusion of a state equal rights amendment (Article 46), a provision which was not adopted at the national level.

The main body of the Maryland Constitution consists of eighteen articles. Article I deals with the right to vote and specifies a number of election procedures. Constitutional amendments and decisions of the U. S. Supreme Court have eliminated many of the restrictions on voting that used to be in effect in some states.[9] For example, as a result of the twenty-sixth amendment to the U. S. Constitution in 1971, the voting age is 18 for all federal, state, and local elections.

The next three articles of the Maryland Constitution parallel the U. S. Constitution, in that they deal with the three branches of govern-

Old Annapolis

ment and establish a system of separation of powers. Article II describes the system by which the governor is elected, specifies his formal powers and responsibilities, and outlines his relationship to the rest of the executive branch. All of these aspects are discussed in Chapter 3.

In Article II, as throughout the Maryland Constitution, there have been many amendments, particularly in recent years. The nature of the constitutional system and its evolution can be illustrated by two of those recent changes with respect to the office of governor. A 1970 amendment created the office of lieutenant governor, a proposal that had been made by the 1967 Constitutional Convention, and was intended to insure greater continuity if the office of governor became vacant.

The Governor's Salary Commission was established by a 1976 amendment. Previously, the governor's salary was specified in the constitution and could be changed only by amendment. This is an example of what many critics have pointed to as an overly specific constitutional provision that does not allow adequate flexibility. The Salary Commission is a means by which the governor's compensation can be periodically adjusted without having to change the constitution.

Article III, the longest in the constitution, concerns the legislative branch. Provisions deal with the election and composition of the bicameral General Assembly, the procedures of the legislative process, the powers of the General Assembly, and the limitations and restrictions on those powers.

There is a great deal of specific detail in the legislative article. There are, for example, sections that deal with the legislative calendar, with the relationship of the General Assembly to local jurisdictions, and with individual rights. Chapter 4 provides a more detailed examination of Maryland's legislature.

Article IV, also long and detailed, describes the state's judicial system. In addition to explaining the selection of judges and the general powers of the court, this article spells out the structure of the state court system and the relationship among its different levels.

The judicial branch, which receives the least public attention, has, in fact been the subject of numerous proposals for constitutional change. The 1967 Constitutional Convention focused considerable attention on the structure of the state court system. Subsequently, some of the proposed reforms to consolidate and simplify the structure of the courts were adopted as amendments to the constitution. Another issue which continues to draw attention and debate is the election of judges.[10] The court system is discussed more fully in Chapter 5.

The Maryland Constitution gets even more detailed and specific in the remaining articles. For example, the next three concern the following, respectively: Attorney-General and State's Attorney; Treasury Department; and Sundry Officers, which refers to County Commissioners.

Article VIII, titled Education, has generated a great deal of controversy recently. Section I specifies that the General Assembly "shall by law establish throughout the State a thorough and efficient System of Free Public Schools; and shall provide by taxation, or otherwise, for their maintenance." This provision is a good example of the difficulties of constitutional interpretation. What is the exact nature of the obligation which this language imposes upon the state?

A 1979 lawsuit argued that the Maryland Constitution, as the result of Article VIII, required the state to provide equal educational opportunity for all students, regardless of where they live. Historically, public education has been financed primarily through local property taxes. As a result, the amounts of money spent on education have varied significantly from jurisdiction to jurisdiction. The lawsuit, *Somerset County, et al* v. *Hornbeck*, argued that those disparities violated the state's obligations under the constitution. A number of other states have had similar lawsuits with court decisions both favoring and rejecting the equal education opportunity argument. In Maryland, a district court judge ruled that the state's school financing system was unconstitutional, but he was overruled by the Court of Appeals in 1983.[11]

The issue of how much money the state should provide for public education and the manner in which it should be distributed remains a highly controversial one. It is an example of those cases where the language of the state constitution highlights controversial issues but lacks the precision to resolve them without ambiguity. Instead, resolution must be found through the political processes established by the Constitution.

Most of the remainder of the Maryland Constitution deals with local government. As is discussed in Chapters 7 and 8, the authority of local governments under our federal system comes entirely by delegation from the states. As a result, some portions of the Maryland Constitution contain precise and detailed descriptions of local powers, ranging from such subjects as Off-Street Parking in Baltimore City to residential financing loans.

In addition, Article XI provides the mechanism by which local governments in Maryland can set up home rule systems. There are actually three different provisions, two variations for counties and one for municipalities. The relationship between the state government and local governments is one of central importance and affects all aspects of public policy. The balance between centralized government and the desire for local control has shifted periodically and, under the Maryland Constitution, can continue to do so.

Conclusion

The details of constitutions generally do not receive a great deal of attention from most citizens. State constitutions, such as Maryland's, are so long and complicated that even serious students of government may be intimidated.

Yet the constitution is the starting point for understanding the workings of government. The constitution establishes certain basic principles which are intended to be permanent, or at least very difficult to change. Most discussions about constitutional provisions focus on individual rights, such as freedom of speech or press, which have been fundamental to our system of government. In addition, however, the portions of the constitution that deal with the structure and powers of government deserve our attention. The way in which government works is significantly affected by the constitution.

Maryland's Constitution has undergone a great deal of change in recent years, even though the proposed new constitution of 1968 was not adopted. The changes have eliminated a number of outdated and cumbersome provisions and have improved the capabilities of government. Further revisions are the subject of constant discussion, which is likely to increase as the 1990 opportunity for a constitutional convention grows nearer. In the meantime, the actual workings of government are determined by how the current constitutional structure is used.

Chapter 3

THE GOVERNOR

"The governor in the American state has become the central figure in state politics and in the state government as a whole. He is no longer the nonentity or subordinate of the legislature as he was in the first state constitutions. Every succeeding major constitutional alteration or revision has succeeded in granting to him powers of a high order. Yesterday, the state legislature occupied the position of power; today, the governor has taken its place."

The above observations come from a book published in 1932 and titled *The Governor of Maryland: A Constitutional Study*.[1] The changes that the author, Charles James Rohr, noted then have been confirmed in the years since 1932. In this chapter, we will look at the powers and functions of the governor, starting with the constitutional basis of the office and moving on to include a description of the role of the governor today. First, however, some general observations about executive leadership in our political system today are necessary as background.

Elected chief executives have, at all levels of government, become the focal point for political leadership. While this observation has been most frequently noted with respect to the presidency, there is growing evidence of the increased power of governors and mayors as well.[2]

The formal authority of chief executives, as defined by the federal and state constitutions and by statutes, has not changed dramatically. Instead, the major shift has come through heightened public expectations about the need for and possibility of executive leadership.

We have concluded that the problems we face often require speed and decisiveness by government in responding. Legislators seem incapable of either; so we have turned increasingly to the chief executive.

Similarly, we have granted that secrecy may also be required, particularly at the national level, and again, we see that capability only in the chief executive.

We have also been able to personalize government by focusing on the chief executive. For most citizens, public affairs do not have a high priority. Government seems complex, and its activities are not always easy to understand. Seeing the chief executive as the symbol and spokesperson for government provides a means for making sense of what government does. The increased role of television in political communications has contributed to this development.

These attitudes result in the expectation that the effectiveness of government will be dependent on the efforts and skills of the chief executive. The rhetoric of political campaigns reflects this idea. So do the observations of most political analysts.

Other actors in the political system, such as legislators, tend to defer to the leadership of the executive. Agreement is certainly not guaranteed, but the executive is usually seen as the appropriate initiator of ideas and proposals. We all look to the chief executive to have a "program" or a response to a particular problem.

On the one hand, these expectations are a source of power for a chief executive. The formal authority of the position is enhanced by our willingness to look to the chief executive for leadership.

At the same time, however, the expectations can become a real burden. If the chief executive fails to solve problems, he or she will be held responsible. Expectations may be unrealistic. Not all problems have solutions. Moreover, the consequences of some of the solutions may be costly, unpleasant, or unpopular.

The focus on the chief executive also obscures the fact that there are many others, both within and outside of government, who have important roles to play. Our constitutional system requires the involvement and participation of different institutions. The appropriate balance between public and private activities is also an important issue.

The observations about chief executives are, necessarily, of a general nature. While built on the foundation of research on the presidency, they certainly have application to governors and mayors as well.[3]

In Maryland, there is no question that public expectations about the role of the governor have changed over time. The office has taken on increased importance and power as we have looked increasingly to it for leadership in the state system of government. The more detailed description of the office, which is presented in the remainder of this chapter, can be best understood in this broader context.

Elections and the Office of Governor

According to the Constitution of Maryland, the governor has to be a resident of the state for at least five years, be a qualified voter, and be at least thirty years old. These are all of the formal requirements to be eligible to be elected governor.

Governors have been elected by the voters of the state since 1837. Prior to that date, the General Assembly selected the governor. Maryland's fourth constitution, adopted in 1867, spells out most of the basic provisions covering the election of the governor today.

Of the fifty-seven people who have been governor of Maryland between 1776 and the present, all have been white males. Since 1869, every governor has been a member of either the Democratic or Republican party (see Table 3-1). An examination of the men who have been elected governor since World War II shows that each one was politically active and held at least one other elective office prior to becoming governor.

Elections for all statewide offices including governor are held every four years in the even-numbered year between presidential elections. As a result of a 1948 amendment to the Maryland Constitution, Maryland governors are limited to two consecutive terms of four years each. Harry Hughes, who had been elected to his second four-year term in 1982, was ineligible to run again in 1986.

The central position of the governor in the state is reflected in the competition for the office. With Governor Hughes completing his second and final term, candidates to succeed him included the Mayor of Baltimore City, the Speaker of the House of Delegates, the Attorney General of Maryland, and the Howard County Executive. Campaign activity started well before the 1986 election year with expenditures totalling

---

Question: Maryland's State Constitution allows the governor to serve no more than two consecutive four year terms in office. Should Maryland's Constitution be amended to permit the governor to serve more than two consecutive terms?

YES	NO	UNDECIDED
22%	64%	14%

Source: Mason-Dixon Opinion Research, Inc., Columbia, Maryland. Maryland Opinion Poll, April 1985.

Table 3-1. GOVERNORS OF MARYLAND, 1869–PRESENT

Name	Term of Office	Political Party
Oden Bowie	1869-1872	Democrat
William Pinkney Whyte	1872-1874	Democrat
James Black Groome	1874-1876	Democrat
John Lee Carroll	1876-1880	Democrat
William T. Hamilton	1880-1884	Democrat
Robert M. McLane	1884-1885	Democrat
Henry Lloyd	1885-1888	Democrat
Elihu E. Jackson	1888-1892	Democrat
Frank Brown	1892-1896	Democrat
Lloyd Lowndes	1896-1900	Democrat
John Walter Smith	1900-1904	Democrat
Edwin Warfield	1904-1908	Democrat
Austin L. Crothers	1908-1912	Democrat
Phillips Lee Goldsborough	1912-1916	Republican
Emerson C. Harrington	1916-1920	Democrat
Albert C. Ritchie	1920-1935	Democrat
Harry W. Nice	1935-1939	Republican
Herbert R. O'Connor	1939-1947	Democrat
William Preston Lane	1947-1951	Democrat
Theodore R. McKeldin	1951-1959	Republican
J. Millard Tawes	1959-1967	Democrat
Spiro T. Agnew	1967-1969	Republican
Marvin Mandel	1969-1979	Democrat
Harry Hughes	1979-1987	Democrat
William Donald Schaefer	1987-	Democrat

several million dollars. The winning candidate, William Donald Schaefer, raised and spent over $3 million.

Vacancies can occur in the office if a governor dies or resigns or is removed from office. The Maryland Constitution provides for an impeachment process by the General Assembly and a means for certifying that the governor is temporarily disabled. Unlike many other states, Maryland has no recall provision by which the voters can remove a governor from office before the end of his or her term.

If there is a vacancy in the office of governor, the lieutenant governor succeeds to the office for the remainder of the term. This position was established by a 1970 amendment to the state constitution. If the office is temporarily vacant, the lieutenant governor becomes acting governor. Should both offices be vacant at the same time, the General Assembly, by a majority vote of all members, selects replacements.

These provisions, which may seem obscure to most citizens, have been used in recent years. When Spiro T. Agnew resigned as governor in 1969 to become Vice President of the United States, the General Assembly selected Speaker of the House of Delegates Marvin Mandel to be governor. That was prior to the 1970 amendment creating the office of lieutenant governor. Mandel was elected to full terms of office by the voters in both 1970 and 1974.

However, Governor Mandel turned the office over to Lieutenant Governor Blair Lee in 1977 after Mandel was convicted of federal criminal charges. Lee served as acting governor through the remainder of Mandel's term.[4]

The salary of the governor as of 1986 was $75,000 per year. Prior to 1976, the salary level was fixed by the state constitution at $25,000, and resulted in the governor being paid considerably less than heads of state agencies or members of the governor's staff. The General Assembly passed legislation in 1976 creating the Governor's Salary Commission, which makes recommendations every four years to the General Assembly on changes in the governor's salary for the next ensuing term of office. The commission has recommended that the governor's salary be increased, effective with the new term starting in January 1987, to $85,000.

There is an official residence, the Governor's Mansion, in Annapolis. The cost of maintaining the residence is included in the state budget. Maryland governors also have an official, state-owned yacht at their disposal, making them the only governors in the nation with this perquisite.

Formal Powers of the Governor

Article II of the Maryland Constitution spells out the formal powers of the governor. A comparison with other states shows that the governor of Maryland clearly falls into the category of having "very strong" formal powers.[5]

First, and of critical importance, the governor has extensive authority with respect to the appointment and removal of key officials in the executive branch of the state government. There is a cabinet system, established by legislation, over which the governor has considerable control and direction. There are fourteen principal departments, for which the governor selects the head, or secretary (see diagram below). Furthermore, a department head may be replaced at the governor's discretion. (See Chapter 6 for a fuller discussion of state agencies.)

The Governor's Mansion in Annapolis

In addition to the appointment of department heads, the governor has several hundred positions in both the executive branch and on various boards and commissions for which individuals are selected. (See Table 3-2 for a sample of gubernatorial appointments.) This list of appointments, known as the "Greenbag," can be an important source of influence for the governor. In the first place, this appointment power enables the governor to place individuals with ties to him or her in key decision-making positions in state government. In addition, the appointments are a means of rewarding supporters as well as of attracting potential supporters.

Prior to 1969, Maryland had some two-hundred and fifty separate departments and agencies within the state government. The creation of the fourteen cabinet-level departments, encompassing most of those agencies, greatly increased the governor's ability to supervise state government. Moreover, Maryland's governor has sweeping authority to

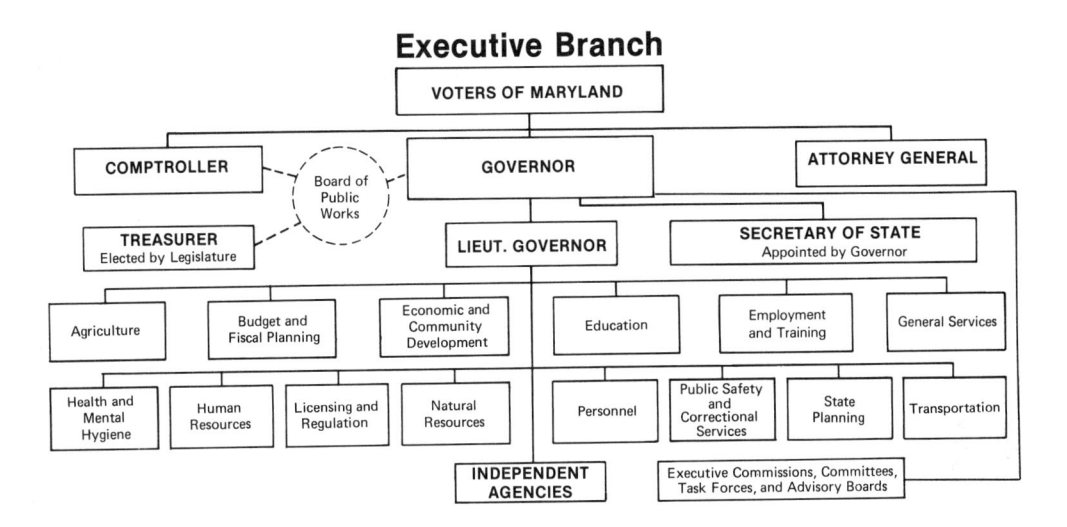

Executive Branch

```
                        VOTERS OF MARYLAND
        ┌───────────────────────┼───────────────────────┐
   COMPTROLLER            GOVERNOR              ATTORNEY GENERAL
        │         Board of      │
                  Public
   TREASURER      Works    LIEUT. GOVERNOR       SECRETARY OF STATE
   Elected by                                    Appointed by Governor
   Legislature
```

| Agriculture | Budget and Fiscal Planning | Economic and Community Development | Education | Employment and Training | General Services |

| Health and Mental Hygiene | Human Resources | Licensing and Regulation | Natural Resources | Personnel | Public Safety and Correctional Services | State Planning | Transportation |

INDEPENDENT AGENCIES

Executive Commissions, Committees, Task Forces, and Advisory Boards

assign agencies that are not among the fourteen cabinet-level departments to one of the principal departments.

The number of independently elected state officials and independent boards and commissions is more limited in Maryland than it is in many other states. The only other state officials elected by the voters are the lieutenant governor, who runs on a ticket with the governor, the state attorney general, and the comptroller.

Another formal power of note is the governor's authority with respect to the state budget. Maryland has what is generally referred to as an "executive" budget system. All state agencies submit their budget requests to the governor who, working through the Department of Budget and Fiscal Planning, decides on the specific amounts that will be requested from the legislature. Thus, the budget process allows the governor to exercise control over the various agencies of state government.

In addition, the state constitution restricts the actions that the legislature may take with respect to the budget. The governor's proposals may not be increased or rearranged between programs and categories. The legislature may only reduce the amounts proposed in the budget. In most years, the budget submitted by the governor has remained largely as it was proposed, with only small changes enacted by the legislature.

The right to veto proposed legislation is another important part of the governor's overall power. If the governor sends a bill back to the legislature, it takes a three-fifths vote in each of the houses to override the veto and to enact the measure in question. Moreover, the governor,

Table 3-2. GUBERNATORIAL APPOINTMENTS, 1986
(REQUIRING SENATE CONFIRMATION)

Position	Number
Afro-American History and Culture	2
Airport Zoning Appeals	4
Amusement Risk Safety Advisory Board	1
Apprenticeship and Training Council	3
Architectural Registration Board	1
Blind Industries and Services of Maryland, Board of Trustees	3
Chesapeake Bay Critical Areas Commission	6
State Board of Chiropractic Examiners	1
State Board for Community Colleges	2
Consumer Council	2
Commission on Correctional Standards	2
State Board of Dental Examiners	1
Maryland Economic Development Corporation, Board of Directors	3
State Board of Education	3
Statewide Master Electrical Licensing Board	3
State Board of Electrologists	1
Emergency Number Systems Board	3
State Board of Environmental Sanitarian Registration	2
State Ethics Commission	1
Maryland Ethnic Heritage Commission	5
Fire-Rescue Education and Training Commission	2
Atlantic States Marine Fisheries Commission	1
Maryland Food Center Authority	2
State Board of Registration for Foresters	1
Handgun Permit Review Board	1
Board of Review of the Department of Health and Mental Hygiene	2
Board of Examiners for Hearing Aid Dealers	1
State Board for Higher Education	2
Maryland Historical Trust, Board of Trustees	3
Commission on Indian Affairs	3
Director of the Juvenile Probationary School for Baltimore County	1
Assistant Directors for the Juvenile Probationary School for Baltimore County	5
Board of Examiners of Landscape Architects	1
Board of Directors for the Maryland Legal Services Corporation	3
Commission on Medical Discipline	1
State Board of Morticians	2
Board of Review of the Department of Natural Resources	2
State Board of Examiners of Nurses	1
State Board of Occupational Therapy Practice	1
State Board of Pharmacy	1

Position	Number
State Board of Commissioners of Practical Plumbing	2
Advisory Council on Prevailing Wage Rates	2
Board of Examiners of Psychologists	3
Maryland Racing Commission	2
Real Estate Commission	2
Board of Directors of the Rental Resource Corporation	11
Maryland Transportation Authority	2
Board of Review of the Department of Transportation	3
Board of Regents of the University of Maryland	4
Maryland Veterans' Home Commission	3
State Board of Veterinary Medical Examiners	1
State Board of Waterworks and Waste Systems Operators	5
State Board of Well Drillers	7

Source: Office of the Secretary of State, Maryland.

unlike the president of the United States, has an item veto for appropriations bills. That is, the governor may reject or disapprove of a portion of an appropriations bill while accepting the remainder of the measure. This gives the governor a detailed control over legislation passed by the General Assembly.

The governor is one of three members of the State Board of Public Works, which has the authority to make all decisions about capital expenditures and state contracts. This body makes many of the most important decisions of state government with respect to specific expenditures.[6] The governor's authority is shared with the state comptroller and the state treasurer, an officer who is appointed by the General Assembly.

There are several other formal powers listed in Article II of the constitution, although they are usually regarded as less important. The governor may convene special sessions of the General Assembly if it is thought necessary. Most recently, Governor Hughes convened the General Assembly in special session to respond to the savings and loan crisis of 1985. The General Assembly is not obliged to take any particular action during a special session. The governor is also the commander in chief of the state militia. While the duty of repelling invasions seems a throwback to a much earlier time, there have been occasions in which state governors have used the national guard to restore order. The last example of this was in February 1983 when the national guard was called in to assist the Baltimore city police during a blizzard.

A meeting of the Board of Public Works

OTHER SOURCES OF GUBERNATORIAL POWER

Studies of modern public chief executives, from presidents to governors to mayors and county executives, have emphasized informal powers and political skills in trying to understand those offices.[7] While all incumbents of a particular office possess the same formal authority, not all have been equally powerful or effective.

This perspective is useful in examining the governor of Maryland. One leading authority describes executive power as the power to persuade rather than the power to command.[8] Certainly the governor of Maryland does not have a monopoly on power within the state and must convince others of the need for cooperation and support.

One important resource available to a governor is the staff. We have seen a dramatic increase in the size of the office of chief executive at all levels of government in the United States. The governor's staff, as of

Table 3-3. THE GOVERNOR'S STAFF

Year	Number
1949-1950	9
1951-1952	11
1953-1954	12
1955-1956	12
1957-1958	13
1959-1960	15
1961-1962	17
1963-1964	20
1965-1966	20
1967-1968	42
1969-1970	44
1971-1972	63
1973-1974	74
1975-1976	76
1977-1978	78
1979-1980	75
1981-1982	93
1983-1984	98
1985-1986	114

Source: Maryland State Archives, *Manual: State of Maryland 1985-1986.*

fiscal 1986, was 114, a sharp increase from the total of 9 in 1950. (See Table 3-3.)

What does the governor's staff do? The most visible staff aides are the press secretary and the members of the governor's legislative office. In addition, there is a program office that includes specialists in such fields as education, transportation, health, and economic development. Governors have different goals and styles; and therefore their staffs will be organized and function in different ways.

In general terms, the governor's staff will gather information, give advice, help the governor communicate both with the rest of state government and the public, and represent the governor at various meetings. Today, any chief executive's office is really an institution composed of many individuals rather than just the office holder. We expect our governor to do a lot of different tasks, and the staff has grown as a means to help carry out those expectations.

A second important source of informal power for the governor is the ability to select issues that the rest of the governmental system will consider. This is a characteristic of all levels of government in the United States today.[9] We look to our chief executives to take the initiative. We expect them—whether they be the president, governor, or mayor—to have a program. We may not always agree with what they have proposed, but we do allow them to define many of the public issues which we will then debate.

The governor does not have total control over the agenda of course. Problems arise that must be dealt with, such as the widespread recognition that the Chesapeake Bay is dangerously polluted and needs to be cleaned up. Other office holders may propose ideas to which the governor is forced to respond. The effort of the Mayor of Baltimore in 1984 to achieve a significant increase in state funding of public education represents an example. Moreover, some governors have been more skillful than others in identifying and defining the issues for public consideration. Nevertheless, governors have the opportunity, if they choose to use it, to initiate proposals.

Third on the list of informal powers is the governor's ability to speak for and to the public as a whole.[10] The governor is elected by all the voters of the state and represents them in a way that no individual member of the General Assembly can. Governors have ready access to the media of the state and can, if they want, communicate their ideas and preferences to the public. Most governors have weekly press conferences and, in addition, are covered by the press whenever they have an announcement to make.

The governor can try to educate and persuade the public of the need for a particular action. Public opinion can, in turn, have a significant influence on the actions of the legislature.

As with the other informal powers, access to media coverage and public attention does not insure that the governor will use this resource effectively. Nor does it prevent other officials from attempting to convince the public to support positions contrary to the governor's.

The Roles of the Governor

What does a governor do? One way of answering this question is to examine the kinds of things that a governor does on a normal day. While no day is really typical, the list of activities may include: meetings with members of the staff as well as department heads; conferences with legislative leaders; visits from members of the general public, either individuals or groups; press conferences; making phone calls and writing letters; and appearing at public functions, some of which are official

Governor Harry Hughes at a press conference

work, others of which are ceremonial. This list does not include time for thinking about problems or time for purely personal and family activities. In addition, the governor may also be traveling, around the state, to Washington, D.C., or to meetings around the country, such as the National Governors' Association. (See Table 3-4.)

A second way to think about the activities of governors is to consider the different roles that they play. While the job of modern governors goes well beyond the formal constitutional requirement of being chief executive of the state government, the management of the state bureaucracy does remain a vital part of their responsibilities.

Being chief executive revolves, in turn, around two primary objectives: the delivery of needed services to the public and a concern about the cost of providing those services. The single most important activity is the budget process. The governor must decide which programs and services are needed, how available financial resources are to be distributed among a variety of competing priorities, and whether additional re-

Table 3-4. THE GOVERNOR'S TIME SCHEDULE[a]

Activity	Column A[b] (in percent)	Column B[c] (in percent)
Managing state government	29	27
Working with the legislature	16	18
Meeting the general public	14	—
Ceremonial functions	14	13
Working with press and media	9	7
Working with federal government	7	7
Working with local government	7	7
Political activities	6	8
Recruiting and appointing	6	8
Miscellaneous activities (staff, interstate, reading, phoning)	16	9

Source: Thad L. Beyle, "The Governor as Chief Legislator," *State Government* (Winter 1978), p. 3. Reprinted with permission of the Council of State Governments, Lexington, Kentucky.

[a] Totals do not add to 100 percent but are averages of the respondents' estimates of the time devoted to the particular activity by the governor.
[b] Percentages based on responses from those scheduling gubernatorial time in 40 states.
[c] Percentages based on responses from governors of 16 states.

sources are needed. This last question, which all governors agree creates the most problems for them, is, in simple terms, whether taxes should be raised.

Recent efforts to reduce the overcrowding in the state's prison system illustrate the choices facing a governor as chief administrator. Both corrections officials and judges in court cases have insisted that more prison facilities are needed. The governor, in responding, must consider not only the cost but conflicting preferences about a desirable location.

A second role of the governor is a policy making one. He or she must, in conjunction with other officials, including members of the legislature, decide on future directions for the state. The public will tend to look to the governor to make proposals to the legislature on how to deal with impending issues. Prominent contemporary examples include: what position the state government should take in the financing and control of public education; what steps the state government can and should take to foster and stimulate economic development; and what transportation systems are desirable and economically feasible.

Governors may be urged to take stands on a wide range of issues. The preceding examples are probably unavoidable for any governor,

The State House in Annapolis

although the specific choices may vary. There are other issues, of concern to different groups of citizens, that governors may or may not choose to involve themselves in. Whether or not the governor gets involved is sometimes crucial for the resolution of the issue. Controversies over handgun regulation, restrictions on abortion, and drunk driving laws are illustrations. In the first two cases governors have been reluctant to take a clear and strong position, and the debates have continued. Maryland has passed a series of new laws on drunk driving with the governor supporting the efforts of lobbying groups to bring about passage.

Governors are also in the position of being governmental intermediaries. In our federal system of government, a large portion of the actual delivery of services to citizens is at the local level. At the same time, the federal government supplies some of the money for these programs as well as some of the regulations. The governor must go to Washington and try to persuade the federal government to provide assistance. Governor Hughes did this in 1984 in discussions with the Environmental Protection Agency about funds for cleaning up the Chesapeake Bay. The state, in fact, has an office and ongoing lobbying effort in Washington, D.C.

The governor must also deal with representatives of other states. This may take the form of direct contact with the governor of another state, as in Governor Hughes' meetings with Charles Robb of Virginia about the Chesapeake Bay. Participation in national organizations, such as the National Governors' Association, is another form of this activity.

Similarly, the governor hears consistently from local officials about their needs and must decide whether the state can provide the requested assistance. State support for the Baltimore Convention Center and for the subway system are examples of local projects being seen as having regional and statewide impact. Requests for state aid for local services and projects are not always supported, however, and these decisions are often made by the governor.

The governor is, in addition to these other roles, a political figure. By definition, the governor is a leading member of one of the major political parties. Possibly excepting the office of United States Senator, most observers would rate the governorship as the highest elective office in the state. The governor may become involved in supporting candidates in elections at both the state and federal level. In addition, Maryland governors, limited by the state constitution to two four-year terms, may aspire to other elective offices after their term as governor.[11]

The political role affects the governor's relationship with the public as well as with other members of the state government. A popular governor will have a greater ability to get things done in the legislature. Similarly, a governor who is seen as effective by the public is more likely to retain public support and popularity. It is this political role that ties all the other activities of the governor together.

Conclusion

The governor is the chief executive of Maryland. While the formal powers of the office are specified in the state constitution, the office has expanded its activities in recent years. The power and effectiveness of the governor are dependent on his ability to use his informal as well as his formal powers.

The governor must work with many other people in state government to carry out the job. The governor's relationship with the General Assembly is a key to understanding the workings of Maryland government. The next chapter presents an examination of the state legislature.

Chapter 4

THE STATE LEGISLATURE OF MARYLAND

Government leadership at all levels in the United States has increasingly come to be exercised by elected chief executives. The expanded scope of government functions, the movement toward greater centralization, and the need for quick and decisive action have all contributed to this pattern. Legislatures are, at times, looked upon as obstacles to progress, and their procedures are often described as unnecessarily cumbersome and unwieldy.

In fact, reservations about legislatures are not entirely new either. More than a century ago, Daniel Webster observed that "No man's house or property is safe when the legislature is in session."[1] A look at state constitutions and local charters shows that legislatures are restricted in a variety of ways, from formal powers, to length of session, to support for carrying out their functions.

There is another side to this picture however. A basic characteristic of American government at all levels is separation of power within government. We divide authority to prevent any individual or institution from operating without restraint or accountability. However much we have looked to executives for leadership, we are still unwilling to turn over all power to a single branch or individual. At the very least, legislatures provide a mechanism for checking the actions of the executive.

In addition, legislatures are still granted significant formal authority within our constitutional system. While the specific powers of legislatures vary, they all have authority over important decisions of government. How they exercise that authority is still a matter of importance to the workings of our system of government.

Moreover, there have been reforms in the operation of legislatures in recent years. The qualifications and skills of people serving in legislatures, the level of professionalism and support, and modifications in legislative procedures have all improved and upgraded the quality of legislatures.[2]

Understanding the modern state legislature requires an examination of the dual role of legislators: on the one hand, serving and representing constituents; and, at the same time, making laws for the state.[3] The representative and law-making functions may not always be compatible or easy to reconcile. The stalemates within legislatures on complex and controversial issues are, at times, more a reflection of the lack of consensus within the community than a result of complicated legislative procedures or the indecisiveness of individual legislators.

A key dilemma of our society today is that the resolution of many issues has a greater impact on some people and groups than on others.[4] If we all agree, for example, that more prison facilities are needed, we still have to decide in whose community they will be built. Similarly, public investment in economic development projects is likely to bring more benefits to some individuals than to others. What is good public policy for the state as a whole may not benefit or may even harm particular areas.

Legislators, whose continued tenure in public office is dependent on the approval of constituents in their particular district, are likely to see the public interest in different ways. That fact is the strength of the representative process, but it also explains why state legislatures have difficulty in exercising policy leadership.

With this general perspective in mind, we can now turn to an examination of the Maryland Legislature.

History

The state legislature of Maryland is among the oldest in the United States. The first meeting was held in 1635, almost one hundred and fifty years before the American Revolution. The state legislature, known as the General Assembly, began as a unicameral or one-house legislature and changed to its present bicameral system in 1650. Originally, members of the House of Delegates were elected for one-year terms, with four delegates from each of the eighteen counties and two each from Annapolis and Baltimore. The Senate had a similar composition, with members being elected for five-year terms, with two senators from each of the counties and one each from Annapolis and Baltimore.

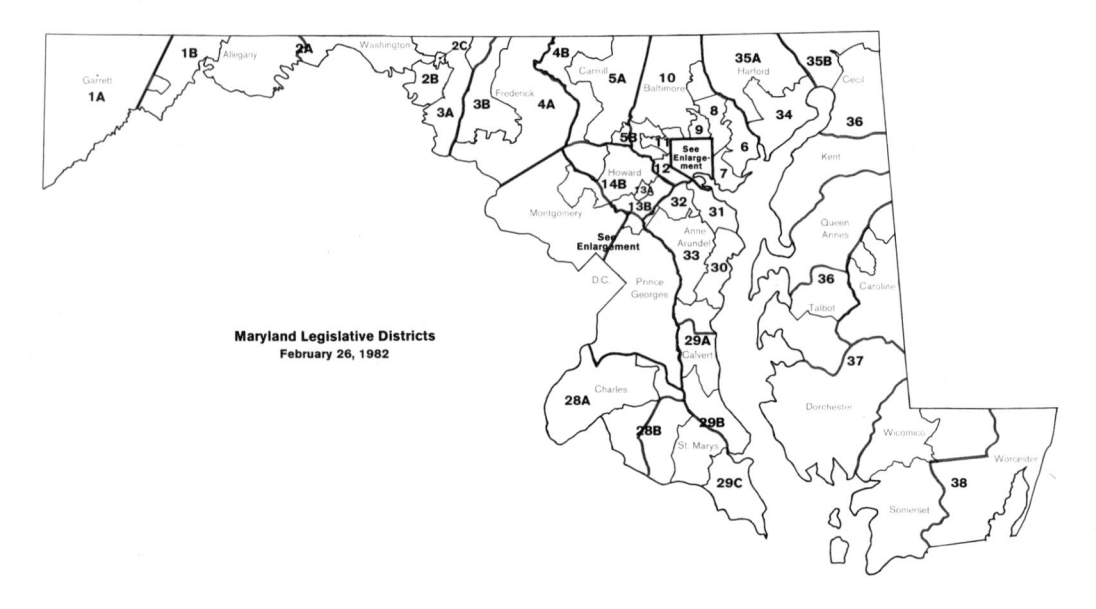

**Maryland Legislative Districts
February 26, 1982**

The House and Senate terms were eventually increased and decreased respectively to a uniform four-year term, with elections held in the even-numbered year between presidential elections. By the mid-nineteenth century, regular sessions were convened every two years. In 1948, the sessions became annual, with a ninety-day session in odd years and a thirty-day session in even years. By 1970, sessions were changed to their present form of ninety days annually. The original legislature met in St. Mary's City and moved to Annapolis in 1695. Sessions have been held in Annapolis continuously since that time. The only exception was during the Civil War when the 1861 session was held in Frederick because the Union Army was occupying Annapolis.

ELECTIONS

Maryland has the sixth largest state legislature in the United States. The Senate and House of Delegates have a total of 188 members. There are forty-seven legislative districts in Maryland, with one senator and three delegates elected from each district. To qualify for office, one must be a resident of the state for at least one year and have lived for at least six months in the district where the election for office is being held. A person must be at least twenty-one years old to be elected to the House of Delegates and at least twenty-five years old to be elected to the Senate.

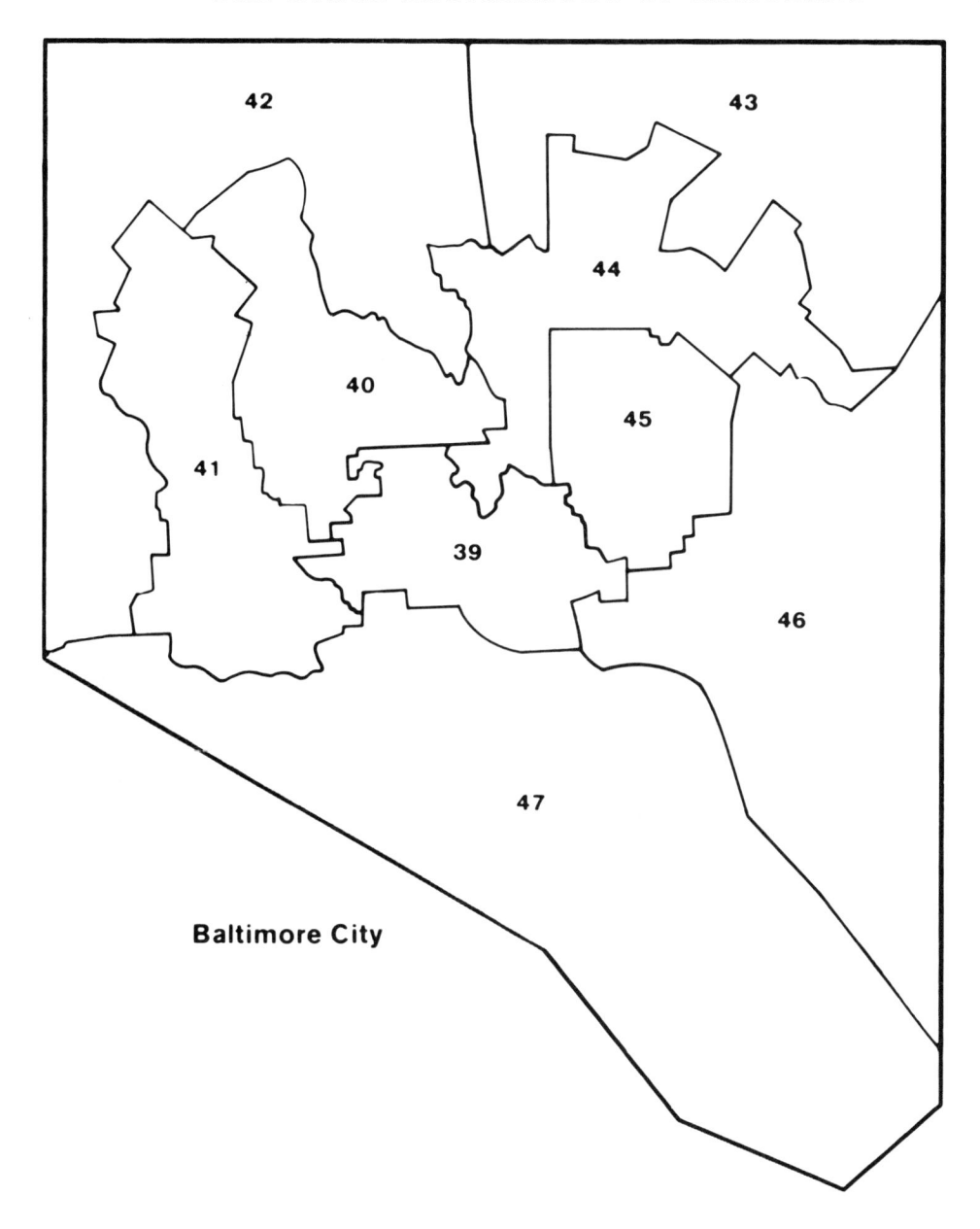

THE STATE LEGISLATURE OF MARYLAND 59

Baltimore City

Montgomery County

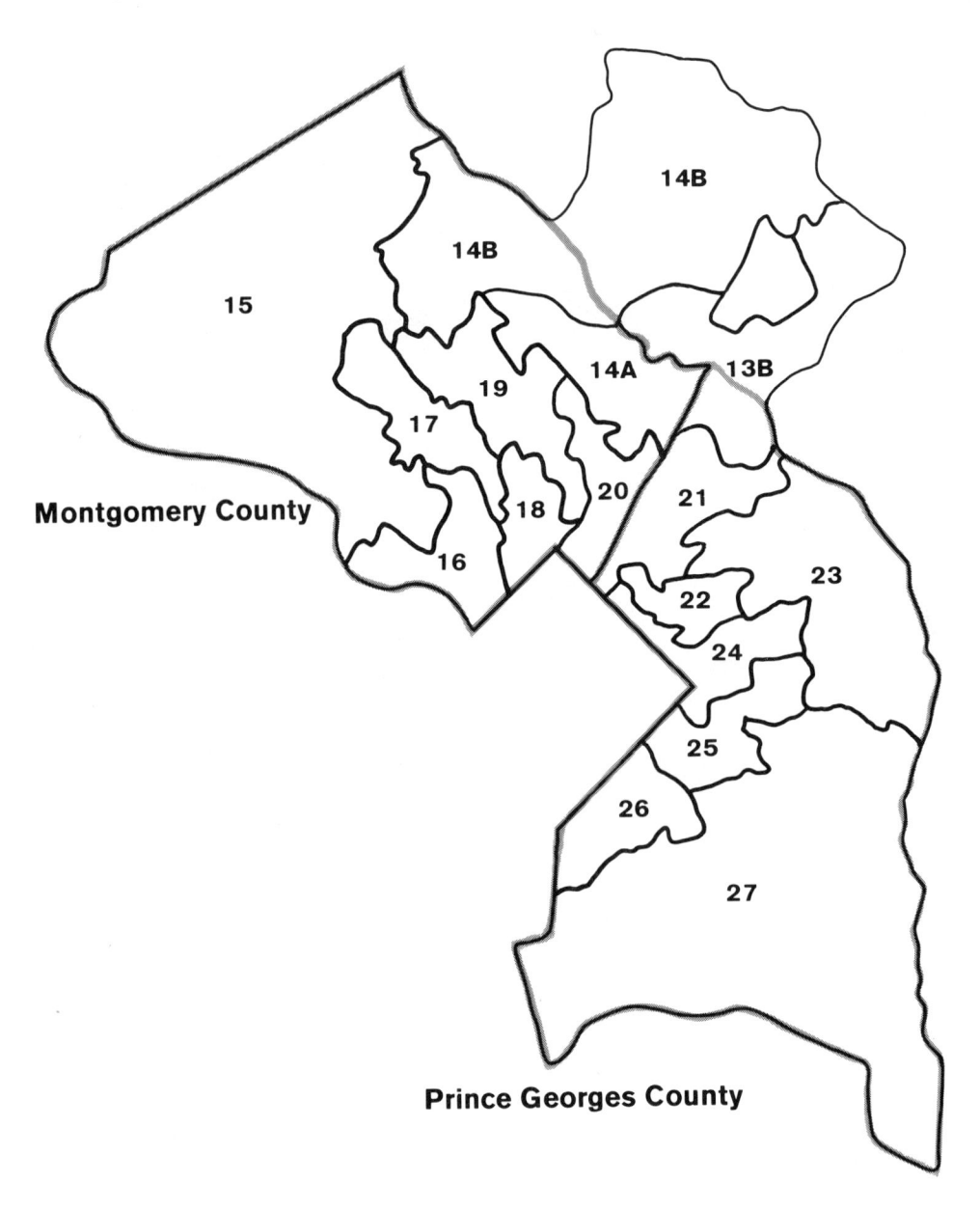

Prince Georges County

If a position is vacated for any reason, it is the governor's duty to appoint a person to the vacated office. The candidate must be of the same political party as the person who vacated the office, and is recommended to the governor by that party's state central committee in the district where the position was vacated.

The forty-seven state legislature districts of Maryland are all approximately equal in population. After each national census, which occurs every ten years, the legislative boundaries are redrawn to reflect shifts in population that have occurred. Under the present system, the governor is responsible for drawing up a reapportionment plan. The General Assembly may either substitute a plan of its own or allow the governor's proposal to take effect.

The issue of reapportionment has been a controversial one in Maryland and the rest of the country. For much of the twentieth century in a number of states including Maryland, legislative boundaries were not revised, resulting in enormous differences in the population of districts. In 1962, the U. S. Supreme Court ruled that reapportionment was required by the U. S. Constitution and that legislative districts had to be substantially equal in population.[5] In Maryland, the General Assembly which convened in January 1967 was the first based upon that principle.

The most recent reapportionment was completed following the 1980 census and took effect in time for the 1982 election. The average population in each legislative district at that time was 89,723.

Characteristics of Legislators

Two characteristics stand out in any examination of the Maryland Legislature. In the first place, approximately 90 percent of the members, all but 19 of the 188, are Democrats (as of 1986). From that perspective, Maryland is clearly a one-party state. Differences of opinion and perspective come from factors other than political party.

The second generalization is that the job of legislator is, for most, a part-time position. The tradition of citizen-legislators is an old one, tied to a period when the work of government and the legislature was more limited than it is today. The growing need to be involved in legislative activity between sessions as well as the incidence of special sessions have put increased pressure on the concept of the part-time legislator.

Being a legislator requires both the desire and interest to serve and the ability to fit the legislative workload requirements into whatever other responsibilities an individual has. For the latter reason, candidates for the legislature have been most often individuals with personal resources as well as flexibility in their schedules, such as lawyers. Significant increases in the salary level in the last ten to fifteen years have made it possible for individuals to devote full time to the legislature. For the legislature elected in 1982, the salary was $21,000. This may start to open up the positions to a broader range of backgrounds and fields.

Interest in being a legislator may be motivated by many different factors.[6] Some individuals see the state legislature as a step on the way to higher elective offices. Others are primarily interested in public policy and service. The ability to combine a part-time legislative position with another career attracts some. A combination of these factors undoubtedly influences many members of the legislature. A more detailed breakdown on the characteristics of the members of the Maryland General Assembly is presented in Table 4-1.

The average senator is white, male, in his fifties and a Democrat. Most senators are either lawyers or businessmen with at least a college degree, and have served more than one term in office. About ten percent of the senators have previous legislative experience in the House of Delegates.

By comparison, the average delegate is also a white male and a Democrat, but on the average is seven years younger than the Senate counterpart. A broader professional representation is found in the House, but the majority are still lawyers, businessmen, or government employees. At least seventy percent of the delegates have a minimum of a bachelor's degree.

State legislatures generally have a fairly high level of turnover. Maryland is no exception to this pattern. In the General Assembly elected in 1982, there were nineteen new senators, or forty percent of the total membership, and fifty first-time delegates, thirty-five percent of the full House.

Organization

The lawmaking activities of the General Assembly center on two basic organizing principles: the key role played by the leadership in the Senate and the House; and the division of much of the work into specialized committees.

The presiding officer in each house of the legislature is elected at the start of each session by a caucus of the majority party and exercises a

THE STATE LEGISLATURE OF MARYLAND

Table 4-1. CHARACTERISTICS OF THE MARYLAND GENERAL ASSEMBLY

Characteristics	Senate Total	Senate Percent	House Total	House Percent
	47		141	
Sex				
Male	44	94	106	75
Female	3	6	35	25
Race				
White	42	89	123	87
Black	5	11	18	13
Other	0		0	
Average Age	51		46	
Professions				
Law	15	32	31	22
Business	18	38	33	23
Education	2	4	24	17
Farming	0		7	5
Government	0		19	14
Health	1	2	5	4
Religion	0		1	—[a]
Full Time Legislator	0		2	1
Other	11	24	19	14
Highest Educational Degree				
High School	4	8	17	12
Some College	8	17	24	17
Bachelor's Degree	12	26	37	26
Post Bachelor's Degree	23	49	63	45
Average Number of Terms	2		1	
1 Term	15	32	51	36
2 Terms	10	21	36	25
3 Terms	10	21	29	20
4 Terms	4	9	15	11
5 Terms	5	11	10	7
Above 5 Terms	3	6	0	0
Prior Elected Experience	28[b]	60	2	1
Party Affiliation				
Democrat	42	89	127	90
Republican	5	11	14	10

Source: *Manual: State of Maryland 1983-1984.*

[a] Under 1 percent
[b] Previous House of Delegates Experience

great deal of influence over the legislative process.[7] The key power that the President of the Senate and the Speaker of the House of Delegates have is that of appointing all committees, including designating the chairman and vice chairman of each.

In addition, the president and the speaker control the schedule by which legislation is considered, generally supervise the proceedings of their respective houses, share responsibility for selecting the directors of the legislative support agencies, and cochair the Legislative Policy Committee, which conducts the work of the legislature between sessions.

As in any leadership position, the power of a senate president or house speaker will depend on the skills of the individual holding the position and the circumstances that he has to deal with. Nevertheless, the formal powers of these leadership positions are considerable.

Much of the review and consideration of laws by the General Assembly, as with most legislatures, is done in committees.[8] In each house, there are a number of standing committees that handle much of the general legislation, and which are subject to change from one session to another. There are also standing committees which deal with nonlegislative matters.

In addition, each house has a series of select committees that review local legislation which has no statewide impact. Select committees are composed of the senators or delegates from the particular jurisdictions involved in the local legislation. Finally, there are joint committees that are concerned with activities of the legislature between sessions, as well as with issues of common interest that are nonlegislative in nature.

At the present time, there are six standing committees in the Senate, eight standing committees in the House, and seven joint committees. Each committee has specific jurisdiction over an area of legislation.

The Senate standing legislative committees, including their principal subject areas are:

    1. The Budget and Taxation Committee

    State operating and capital budgets, including revenues and expenditures; supplementary appropriations bills; state and county bond authorizations; legislative budgetary procedures; property assessments and taxation; and creation of judgeships.

    2. The Economic and Environmental Affairs Committee

    Licensing and regulation of businesses and labor in general, including business, health, and related occupations and pro-

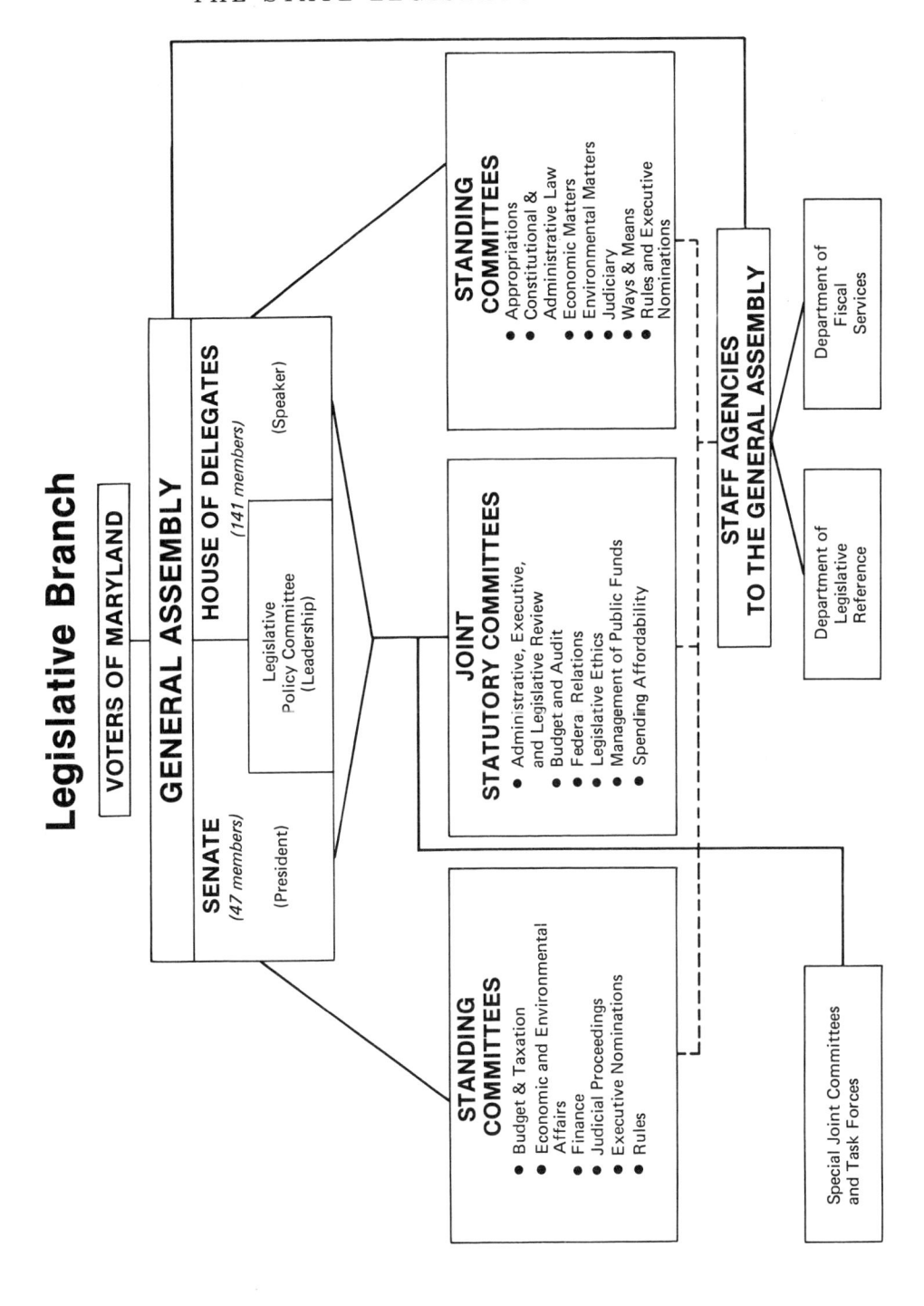

THE STATE LEGISLATURE OF MARYLAND

Legislative Branch

VOTERS OF MARYLAND

GENERAL ASSEMBLY

SENATE (47 members) (President)

HOUSE OF DELEGATES (141 members) (Speaker)

Legislative Policy Committee (Leadership)

STANDING COMMITTEES (Senate)
- Budget & Taxation
- Economic and Environmental Affairs
- Finance
- Judicial Proceedings
- Executive Nominations
- Rules

STANDING COMMITTEES (House)
- Appropriations
- Constitutional & Administrative Law
- Economic Matters
- Environmental Matters
- Judiciary
- Ways & Means
- Rules and Executive Nominations

JOINT STATUTORY COMMITTEES
- Administrative, Executive, and Legislative Review
- Budget and Audit
- Federal Relations
- Legislative Ethics
- Management of Public Funds
- Spending Affordability

Special Joint Committees and Task Forces

STAFF AGENCIES TO THE GENERAL ASSEMBLY
- Department of Legislative Reference
- Department of Fiscal Services

fessions; alcoholic beverages; natural resources; agriculture and land preservation; energy; election laws; veterans affairs; mobile homes; fire prevention; education programs; procurement; environmental health; local government affairs; and state government organization, procedures, and administrative law.

3. The Finance Committee

Transportation; health and welfare matters; state personnel; pensions and retirement; unemployment insurance; workmen's compensation; horse racing; banking and financial institutions; credit regulation and consumer financing; economic and community development; insurance; utility regulation; and labor and employment.

4. The Judicial Proceedings Committee

Judicial administration and court structure; constitutional amendments; legal profession; criminal and civil laws, and penalties and procedures; legal rights and immunities; corrections; juvenile justice; family law; ethics; commercial code; real property; landlord-tenant laws; trusts and estates; public safety; law enforcement organization and personnel, equal rights and opportunities; and vehicle laws.

In addition the Senate has an Executive Nominations Committee that reviews all appointments made by the governor to executive branch positions.

The House of Delegates has a similar committee structure. The six standing legislative committees in the House, with their primary responsibilities, are:

1. The Committee on Appropriations

State operating and capital budgets; supplementary appropriation bills; state and county bond authorizations; correctional institutions; higher education institutions; legislative budgetary procedures; and state personnel and pension matters.

2. The Committee on Constitutional and Administrative Law

State and local government operations; reorganization, structure, and procedures of executive and administrative departments and agencies; utility regulation; ethics and election laws; education structure and curricula; public employee bargaining; workmen's compensation; antidiscrimination and civil rights; U. S. and State Constitutional amendments; and congressional and legislative redistricting.

3. The Committee on Economic Matters

Licensing and regulation of businesses and labor in general, including related occupations and professions; commercial law; insurance and banking regulation; economic development; housing programs; unemployment insurance; consumer protection; and alcoholic beverages.

4. The Committee on Environmental Matters

Regulation of natural resources and environmental matters, including related occupations and professions; energy; agriculture; Chesapeake Bay matters; land use planning and zoning; and health and mental health matters.

5. The Committee on the Judiciary

Judicial administration and court structure; legal profession; criminal and civil laws, penalties, immunities, and procedures; corrections; juvenile justice; marriage and divorce; business structures; real estate transactions; landlord-tenant relations; trusts and estates; motor vehicle laws; and public safety.

6. The Committee on Ways and Means

State and local taxation matters, including assessments and tax credit programs; creation of new state programs and services; education finance; funding of health, welfare, and transportation programs; and lottery and horse racing.

The two nonlegislative standing committees in the House are the Committee on Rules and Executive Nominations and the House Protocol Committee.

The two houses end up reviewing the same material. The committee structures parallel each other, but the specific areas of legislation are divided up differently in the House and the Senate. One reason for this is that the 47 senators must cover the same legislative agenda as the 141 delegates. Thus, there tends to be more specialization in the House than in the Senate. The number and specific responsibilities of the legislative committees have changed frequently and are not tied to any particular rules or requirements. The Speaker of the House and the President of the Senate have the authority to revise the committee structures of their respective houses from session to session.

Of the seven joint committees, the most important and powerful is the Legislative Policy Committee. This committee, which dates back to 1939, oversees all legislative activities between sessions. It was originally called the Legislative Council, and was composed of the leaders of the Senate and House. Gradually, both the role and size of the committee expanded as activities between legislative sessions grew. In 1976, the Legislative Council was abolished and the Legislative Policy Committee was established. Its major responsibilities are to conduct studies in areas where legislation may be needed, to assist in creating the agenda for the regular legislative session, and to oversee the general functioning of the legislature.

The other joint committees of the General Assembly (in addition to the Legislative Policy) are:

1. Administrative, Executive, and Legislative Review
2. Budget and Audit
3. Legislative Ethics
4. Federal Relations
5. Spending Affordability
6. Management of Public Funds

One other kind of committee used by legislatures is the conference committee. If the House and the Senate pass different versions of the same bill, a conference committee made up of members from each house is established to try to resolve the differences and to agree upon a single bill.

Legislative Support

The General Assembly has support services available to help it carry out its duties. The Department of Legislative Reference is responsible for the preparation and processing of all bills introduced in the General Assembly. The Department also supplies research and policy analyses for use by legislators and committees. In addition, there is a Legislative Reference Library which contains material relevant to the legislative process.

The Department of Fiscal Service is the principal financial service arm of the General Assembly. Its main activities include: review of the state operating and capital budget, including analysis and recommendations to the General Assembly; examination of tax alternatives and of the fiscal impact of state programs; and postaudits of all state agencies.

The Legislative Process

The legislative workload of the Maryland General Assembly is a heavy one and has remained relatively constant in recent years. Between 1970 and 1985, legislators have introduced about twenty-five hundred to

Table 4-2. LEGISLATIVE ACTIVITY IN THE MARYLAND GENERAL ASSEMBLY

Year	Total Number of Bills Introduced	Number of Senate Bills Introduced	Number of House Bills Introduced	Total Number of Bills Signed by the Governor	Total Number of Bills Vetoed by the Governor
1960	298	127	171	118	4
1970	2427	888	1539	740	27
1975	2868	1160	1708	898	91
1980	3139	1085	2054	879	93
1981	3041	1127	1914	814	95
1982	3052	1130	1922	871	124
1983	2456	900	1556	687	64
1984	2813	1073	1740	798	84
1985	2601	878	1723	789	93

Source: Department of Legislative Reference.

three thousand bills a session, with close to eight hundred each year being enacted into law. (See Table 4-2.)

The process of enacting a bill into a law is fairly uniform throughout the states. Depending on the type and complexity of the bill introduced, the process can be swift or lengthy. To begin the process: an idea takes form and is developed by the interested parties, which may include legislators, the governor, lobbyists, citizens' groups, and others. The idea is then drafted into proposed legislation, often with assistance by the Department of Legislative Reference. The bill is introduced in the House or Senate by the legislator or legislators who are sponsoring the bill. There the bill has its first reading and is assigned to an appropriate committee, depending on the subject matter. The committee discusses the bill, does further study as necessary, holds hearings, and then reports back to the chamber where the bill originated. If a bill is reported out of committee, there is a second reading, a committee report, and then floor consideration. This stage consists of debate, the possibility of amendment, and, finally, a vote. If the bill passes, it is printed for the third reading.

After a bill is read for the third and final time, it is sent to the other house for consideration. It must go through the same process in the second chamber as it did in the first one. If the second house makes changes in the proposed legislation, there are two possible means of reconciling the differences. The bill may be sent back to the first chamber where a vote can be taken to accept the modified version. Alternatively, a

The House of Delegates

conference committee of members from each house can be set up to work out a new, compromise bill. This version must then go to each of the houses for a favorable vote.

After a bill has passed both houses in identical form, it is sent to the governor, who must either sign or veto the bill. If the legislature is still in session, the governor must act within six days. Following adjournment of a session, a bill must be sent to the governor within twenty days. The governor then has thirty days in which either to sign the measure into law or to veto it.

A bill vetoed during the session is considered by the legislature immediately. Other vetoes are taken up at the start of the next legislative session. A bill vetoed in the last, that is, fourth, year of the legislature, cannot be overridden. A three-fifths vote in each house is required to override a veto by the governor, and is quite rare. The governor has an

THE STATE LEGISLATURE OF MARYLAND

The Maryland Senate

item veto for appropriations bills; that is, he may reject a portion of a bill. On the other hand, he may not veto either the budget bill or a proposed constitutional amendment.

The effective date for new laws is included in the bill, but, under the state constitution, that date may not be before June 1 following the legislative session. Most legislation takes effect on July 1, which is the beginning of the state's new fiscal year. Emergency bills, which require a three-fifths majority in each house for passage, go into effect immediately.

Procedures

The business of the General Assembly is conducted through both formal and informal procedures.[9] The Committee on Rules, Organization, and Procedures in the Senate and the Rules and Executive Nomina-

THE PROGRESS OF A BILL

First Chamber: First Reading → Referral to Committee → Second Reading → Third Reading

Second Chamber: First Reading → Referral to Committee → Second Reading → Third Reading (final passage)

Consideration in Chamber which originated Bill → Conference Committee (only when necessary) → TO GOVERNOR

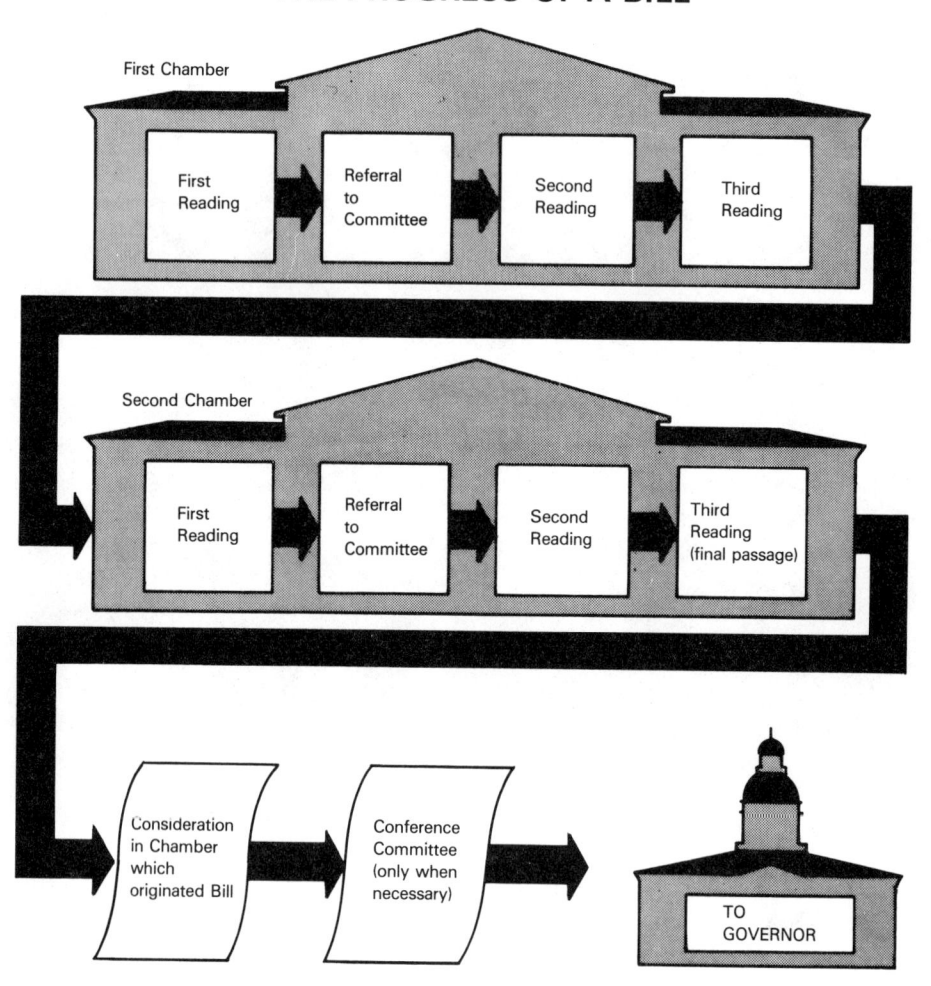

The progress of a bill

tions Committee and the Protocol Committee in the House of Delegates oversee and make recommendations to change and update the procedures of the General Assembly. The formal procedures of business are fairly similar between the two chambers. Parliamentary procedure is followed, using Mason's Manual.

The proceedings of the General Assembly also depend on informal practices, which are the product of traditions and long standing customs. Political parties play a role in this process, but with less influence than in the past. Party caucuses, held prior to the opening of the session, vote on the Speaker and the President of the General Assembly and the minority leaders. Each caucus also decides on its legislative agenda and priorities for the session. The decisions of the caucuses are not binding on the members, but they do reflect what each party feels are important issues for the legislature to address during the upcoming session.

POWERS OF THE GENERAL ASSEMBLY

According to the Maryland Constitution, the General Assembly has the power to pass such laws as are necessary for the welfare of the state. It also has the authority to legislate for counties not having home rule and for special taxing areas. In addition, the General Assembly may propose amendments to the Constitution.

In fact, while the Constitution does enumerate certain specific powers of the legislature, the general interpretation by the courts is that both the Maryland and the U. S. Constitution are primarily a series of restrictions or limitations on what are otherwise unlimited powers.[10] The list of limitations is substantial however.

Individual rights, such as freedom of speech, are in fact prohibitions against governmental action. The U. S. Bill of Rights, the Maryland Declaration of Rights, and sections of the main body of both of those documents contain specific restrictions. Indeed, much of Article III of the Maryland Constitution explains what the legislature is not allowed to do.

When we turn to the actual functioning of government, the role of the legislature is also limited. The single most important action of state government is the development of a budget. Maryland has what is known as an executive budget. The budget is originated by the executive department and submitted to the General Assembly for approval. At the beginning of each legislative session, the governor presents the highlights of the budget, emphasizing new measures or programs in his Budget Message to the General Assembly. By law, the state budget must be balanced between expenditures and revenues. The General Assembly has limited formal authority in the budget process. It cannot increase appropriations, nor shift money between programs. Only after the budget is passed by the legislature can supplemental appropriations bills be considered. All supplemental bills introduced must include revenue measures to finance the proposed additions to the budget. If the General Assembly does not pass the budget bill by the eighty-third day of the session, the governor may extend the regular session by thirty days to complete work on the budget.

The legislature does have some means to influence the development of the budget. The governor has periodic meetings with the Speaker of the House, the President of the Senate, and key committee members to discuss the legislature's priorities for the state budget. While Maryland governors are under no obligation to include the legislature's preferences, they are aware that they need the support of the legislature in order to pass the budget bill. Although the legislature's formal role in the budget process is limited, it does have the ability to influence the final product through informal mechanisms and to persuade the executive to alter or adjust the budget.

Even with the limitations on its powers, the legislature is able to have an impact on important issues. Spending of public funds, including capital construction, the extent and level of state governmental services, regulation of business and industry, state criminal laws, and support for economic development are examples of critical areas in which the decisions of the General Assembly make a substantial difference.

Specific issues in each of these categories are frequently considered by the General Assembly. The initiation of proposals may come from many different sources but the ultimate authority and responsibility reside with the legislature. How much money should be spent by the state on the public school system and how should that money be distributed? What level and form of assistance should the state provide to Baltimore City? What should the laws be with respect to drunk driving? What kind of regulation of the banking industry is needed? All of these questions, which have a direct and significant effect on large numbers of Maryland citizens, have been considered by the General Assembly in recent years. Many are the kinds of issues that are not resolved by a single action, but require continuous reevaluation.

Proposed legislation in any of these areas can be affected by a number of different factors. The role of the governor—whether or not an active position on an issue is taken and how skillfully the action is taken—is of great importance. The chief participants within the legislature include the Senate President, the House Speaker, and the relevant committee chairpersons. Depending on the subject, a few key legislators may be very influential with their colleagues.

In addition, the actions of the legislature are affected by outside pressures. There are issues on which public opinion may be important. This impact is most likely if there are organized groups working to persuade the legislators to take a particular action. These organized efforts may range from a group of citizens who go to Annapolis once

Citizens organizing to influence the political process

during a legislative session to voice their opinion on an issue, to individuals who organize an effort over an entire legislative session to bring about particular action, to those organized interests who are present and active from one legislative session to the next.

This latter group are referred to as lobbyists. State law requires anyone who is paid more than five hundred dollars or who spends more than one hundred dollars in trying to influence the General Assembly, to register with the State Ethics Commission. Table 4-3 provides more information about lobbyists in Maryland. As the figures show, a number of lobbyists are paid very large amounts of money for their efforts, far more, for example, than the salary of the legislators whom they are trying to influence.

Some critics contend that lobbyists may dominate or have excessive influence on the actions of the General Assembly.[11] Activities such as fund raising by lobbyists for political candidates are cited as raising

Table 4-3. LOBBYISTS REGISTERED IN 1985

Number of Lobbyists—Maryland Legislature 286
Number of Organizations Represented 339

Top Five Lobbyists by Number of Clients

1. Bruce C. Bereano	34 Clients
2. Ira C. Cooke	17 Clients
3. James J. Doyle, Jr.	15 Clients
4. Franklin Goldstein	11 Clients
5. Maxine Adler	10 Clients

Top Five Lobbyists by Fees Earned

1. Bruce C. Bereano	$328,811
2. Franklin Goldstein	231,757
3. James J. Doyle, Jr.	220,207
4. Ira C. Cooke	212,830
5. Devin J. Doolan	134,863

Breakdown—Number of Lobbyists by Number of Clients

251 Lobbyists Representing 1 Client Each
15 Lobbyists Representing 2 Clients Each
4 Lobbyists Representing 3 Clients Each
5 Lobbyists Representing 4 Clients Each
1 Lobbyist Representing 5 Clients Each
2 Lobbyists Representing 6 Clients Each
1 Lobbyist Representing 7 Clients Each
2 Lobbyists Representing 8 Clients Each
1 Lobbyist Representing 10 Clients Each
1 Lobbyist Representing 11 Clients Each
1 Lobbyist Representing 15 Clients Each
1 Lobbyist Representing 17 Clients Each
1 Lobbyist Representing 34 Clients Each

Source: State Ethics Commission, *Report of Registered Lobbyists*, 1985.

conflict of interest problems. On the other hand, lobbyists may provide useful information which helps legislators in understanding issues and how the issues affect different groups. Deciding what restrictions on lobbying should be enacted has been a controversial matter in the past and remains so today.

> **Question:** How would you rate the performance of the Maryland General Assembly during the 1985 legislative session; excellent, pretty good, only fair, or poor?
>
> | EXCELLENT | GOOD | FAIR | POOR | UNDECIDED |
> |-----------|------|------|------|-----------|
> | 5% | 30% | 31% | 6% | 28% |
>
> Source: Mason-Dixon Opinion Research, Inc., Columbia, Maryland. Maryland Opinion Poll, April 1985.

CONCLUSION

Legislatures are frequently the subject of criticism. Yet, they have significant authority and the ability to make substantial differences in the lives of most citizens.

While the General Assembly of Maryland may not have the ability to provide sustained policy leadership, it still does have an important role to play. The legislature does provide a forum for the public to express opinions on important issues, and it does offer an alternative to the executive's perspective on public policy. The General Assembly's representative function remains an essential one, even if its lawmaking role may at times be limited.

Chapter 5

THE COURTS AND THE JUDICIAL SYSTEM

The judicial branch of government is responsible for dealing with issues of great importance. The results of court proceedings, whether for criminal or civil cases, have a direct and significant impact on the public. The judicial branch is, in our system of government, coequal with the executive and the legislature. Yet, the workings of the judicial system are not well known to most citizens.

Courts are responsible for the legal resolution of disputes between individuals, for the adjudication of criminal statutes, and for the interpretation of laws. We are inclined to think of judges and the court system as nonpolitical, but the actions of the judicial process clearly have an impact on the political system.

The judicial branch receives less regular coverage from the media than other portions of government, but there are times when court actions are the subject of intense interest. Judges, for the most part, do not seek press attention in the same way that other elected officials do, but their responsibilities may attract it anyway. In some states, television cameras are allowed in courtrooms, thereby increasing public access to the judicial process. Trials of well-known public figures and of crimes that outrage the community are likely to receive coverage. In addition, public discussion often focuses on apparent patterns of judicial decision making, such as strict interpretation of the rights of criminal defendants.

On occasion, courts are asked to intervene in disputes between the other branches of government. The U. S. Supreme Court ended up playing a major role in the Watergate controversy in 1974.[1] The issue of legislative apportionment has been in the courts constantly since 1962.[2]

The question of the state's responsibility with respect to the funding of public education has been taken to the courts. Individuals often go to court to challenge the authority of the legislative and executive branches of government to take particular actions.

The relationship between individuals in our society has been increasingly the subject of court cases as well. Some critics argue, in fact, that American society has become much too litigious, that is, individuals are inclined to settle disputes by resorting to lawsuits rather than considering other means of resolving their difficulties.

Whether the voluntary resort to legal remedies is excessive or not, many citizens find themselves required to utilize lawyers and the legal system to pursue their objectives. Examples include: purchasing of a home; divorce, child custody, and property settlement issues; and the establishment of wills and estate planning. And, these examples do not touch upon the wide variety of business-related encounters which many people have with the legal system.

As this introduction suggests, the impact of the judicial system is significant. For the remainder of the chapter we will explain the structure and operations of that system in Maryland. It is a system that involves both state and local governments in its operation.

Organization of the Court System

The judicial branch of Maryland is divided into four levels, arranged in a hierarchical structure. Table 5-1 shows this organization.

DISTRICT COURT

At the base of the system is the District Court, created in 1970 to replace the miscellaneous system of trial magistrates, people's, and municipal courts which existed prior to that.

The District Court is divided into twelve geographical subdivisions with at least one judge in each subdivision. There is a Chief Judge of the Court who appoints administrative judges to each of the twelve districts with the approval of the Chief Judge of the Court of Appeals. The Chief Judge also appoints administrative clerks and commissioners for each district. These clerks and commissioners perform such duties as setting bail and issuing arrest warrants.

The jurisdiction of the District Court extends into both criminal, including motor vehicles, and civil areas. This jurisdiction is limited by both monetary and time-imprisonment restrictions. The District Court

Table 5-1. THE MARYLAND JUDICIAL SYSTEM

```
                        COURT OF APPEALS
                        Chief Judge and
                          6 associates

                     COURT OF SPECIAL APPEALS
                        Chief Judge and
                         12 associates

                         CIRCUIT COURTS
```

FIRST CIRCUIT	SECOND CIRCUIT	THIRD CIRCUIT	FOURTH CIRCUIT	FIFTH CIRCUIT	SIXTH CIRCUIT	SEVENTH CIRCUIT	EIGHTH CIRCUIT
Dorchester Somerset Wicomico Worcester	Caroline Cecil Kent Queen Anne's Talbot	Baltimore Harford	Allegany Garrett Washington	Anne Arundel Carroll Howard	Frederick Montgomery	Calvert Charles Prince George's St. Mary's	Baltimore City
(6 Judges)	(6 Judges)	(17 Judges)	(6 Judges)	(15 Judges)	(15 Judges)	(19 Judges)	(23 Judges)

ORPHANS' COURTS
All political subdivisions except Harford and Montgomery Counties

THE DISTRICT COURT

CHIEF JUDGE

DISTRICT 1	DISTRICT 2	DISTRICT 3	DISTRICT 4	DISTRICT 5	DISTRICT 6	DISTRICT 7	DISTRICT 8	DISTRICT 9	DISTRICT 10	DISTRICT 11	DISTRICT 12
Baltimore City	Dorchester Somerset Wicomico Worcester	Caroline Cecil Kent Queen Anne's Talbot	Calvert Charles St. Mary's	Prince George's	Montgomery	Anne Arundel	Baltimore	Harford	Carroll Howard	Frederick Washington	Allegany Garrett
(23 Judges)	(4 Judges)	(6 Judges)	(3 Judges)	(10 Judges)	(10 Judges)	(6 Judges)	(12 Judges)	(3 Judges)	(5 Judges)	(4 Judges)	(3 Judges)

holds exclusive jurisdiction in criminal cases when the penalty is fewer than three years imprisonment and the fine is less than $2,500. The jurisdiction in civil cases is exclusive when the fine is less than $2,500. The District Court also exercises concurrent jurisdiction with the Circuit Court in civil cases when the fine is above $2,500, but less than $10,000,

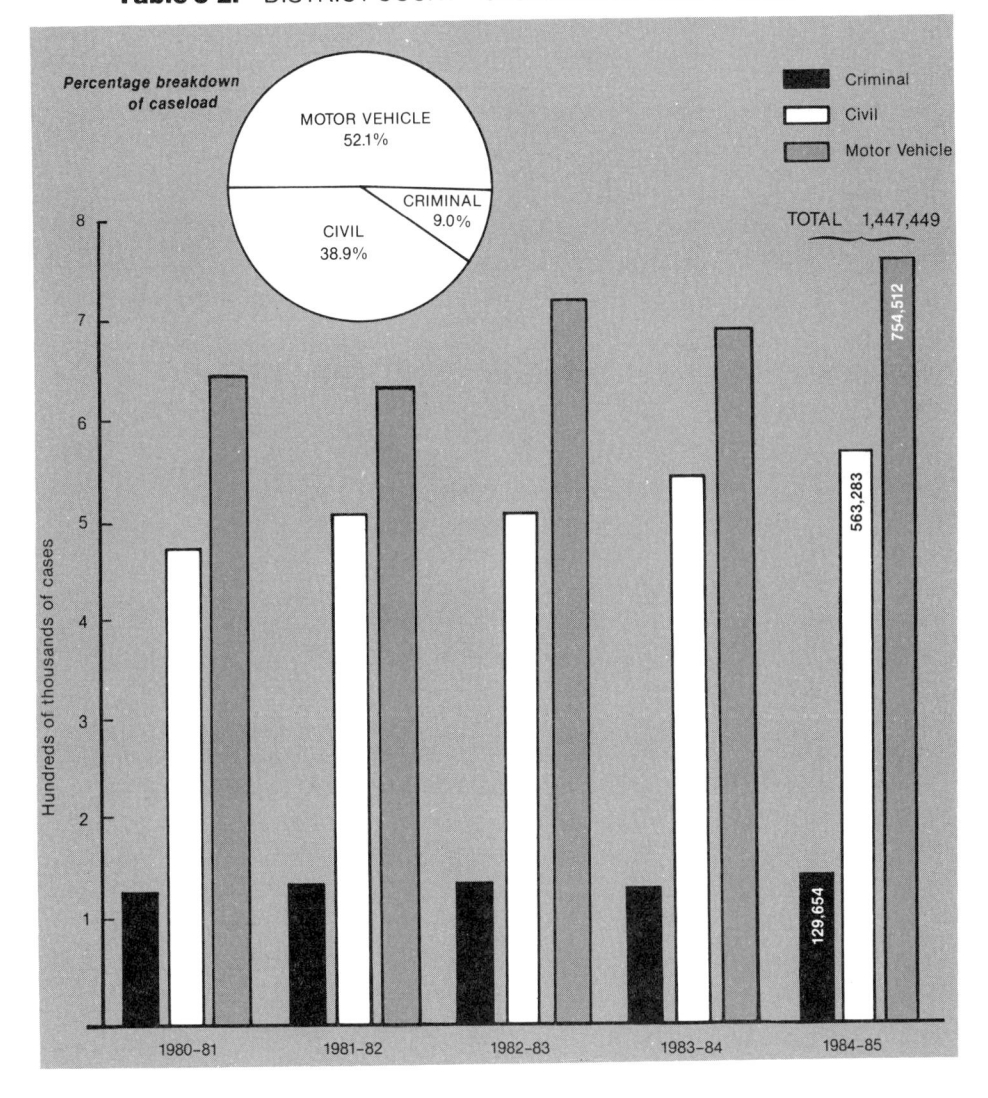

Table 5-2. DISTRICT COURT—CASELOAD BY FISCAL YEAR

and in certain criminal cases. If a person desires to have a jury trial, he or she must proceed to the Circuit Court level.

The total number of cases filed or processed in the District Court in fiscal 1985 was 1,447,449 (see Table 5-2). The largest number of cases filed or processed was in the area of motor vehicle violations (754,512) followed by civil suits (563,283), and finally criminal acts (129,654).

Civil cases have shown the greatest increase in recent years, climbing an average of 25,000 to 30,000 cases over each of the past five

Table 5-3. FIVE-YEAR COMPARATIVE TABLE MOTOR VEHICLE AND CRIMINAL CASES PROCESSED AND CIVIL CASES FILED IN THE DISTRICT COURT, FISCAL 1981–FISCAL 1985

	1980–81[a,b]	1981–82	1982–83	1983–84	1984–85[c]
DISTRICT 1					
Baltimore City	282,352	293,947	317,645	317,274	330,641
DISTRICT 2					
Dorchester	8,006	6,816	6,653	8,324	9,257
Somerset	6,347	6,623	6,381	6,114	6,026
Wicomico	22,289	21,562	24,590	25,122	25,060
Worcester	18,360	14,959	16,528	16,716	16,790
DISTRICT 3					
Caroline	4,763	4,663	4,353	5,298	9,053
Cecil	26,716	25,115	30,882	28,145	33,197
Kent	3,860	4,450	4,089	4,046	4,938
Queen Anne's	7,162	8,022	9,097	8,145	7,667
Talbot	7,993	7,796	8,976	8,171	9,988
DISTRICT 4					
Calvert	7,631	8,340	10,452	10,339	9,438
Charles	13,724	14,475	13,986	17,782	16,406
St. Mary's	9,303	10,020	9,974	8,675	11,251
DISTRICT 5					
Prince George's	250,362	248,058	279,523	260,429	246,377
DISTRICT 6					
Montgomery	153,278	169,797	178,752	174,031	195,906
DISTRICT 7					
Anne Arundel	76,466	79,610	77,230	87,925	97,685
DISTRICT 8					
Baltimore	215,654	190,002	194,513	203,471	226,227
DISTRICT 9					
Harford	34,338	34,199	37,735	38,235	38,954
DISTRICT 10					
Carroll	12,588	12,121	15,215	14,542	18,387
Howard	39,332	44,572	48,645	46,960	46,120
DISTRICT 11					
Frederick	30,426	30,248	32,432	33,508	36,787
Washington	26,558	26,776	27,473	26,695	29,181
DISTRICT 12					
Allegany	13,225	14,022	13,998	13,440	14,027
Garrett	5,067	4,935	5,568	6,219	8,086
STATE	1,275,800	1,281,128	1,374,690	1,369,606	1,447,449

[a] Criminal figures are not available for the months of July and August 1980 for all jurisdictions and for Baltimore City for September 1980 as well. Above statistics have been adjusted by District Court personnel to reflect comparable annual totals.

[b] These figures have been adjusted and are not consistent with previous 1980–81 figures.

[c] The civil rules changes effective July 1, 1984, resulted in the change in the method of compiling the number to be included as "other filings," beginning with FY 1985. The attachments before judgment, confessed judgments, and replevin actions are reported as "other filings." However, supplementary proceedings are no longer included.

years. Landlord and tenant cases amount to approximately seventy-three percent of the civil case total. Both of the other categories, criminal and motor vehicle, have fluctuated.

The twelve districts vary significantly in case load. Table 5-3 shows this variation.

CIRCUIT COURT

The next level in the judicial hierarchy is the Circuit Court. Yet, in fact, the Circuit Court exercises original jurisdiction in a broad range of categories, including all trials by jury, and civil and criminal cases with penalties above the limits for the District Court. The Circuit Court also decides appeals from the District Court and from certain administrative agencies such as the Departments of Personnel, Taxation and Assessment, and Zoning Appeals.

There are eight geographical circuits. Each of the first seven circuits contains two or more counties. The Eighth Judicial Circuit consists of Baltimore City and, as of January 1, 1983, incorporates the former Supreme Bench of Baltimore City. The Chief Judge of the Court of Appeals appoints an administrative judge for each circuit who is, in turn, assisted by county administrative judges.

The caseload for the Circuit Court, which is shown in Table 5-4, can be divided into three categories: civil, juvenile, and criminal cases. Here again, there has been a steady increase in all three areas. The distribution of cases for each circuit varies across the state. Table 5-5 shows these comparisons including a further breakdown of types of cases in each category.

COURT OF SPECIAL APPEALS

The Court of Special Appeals, which was created in 1966, is Maryland's intermediate appellate court. The Court of Special Appeals has thirteen members, one from each of the first five Appellate Judicial circuits, two from the Sixth Appellate Judicial Circuit (Baltimore City), and six from the state at large. Judges usually sit as a three-member panel to hear cases, but may, in certain situations, all be involved in the review of a case.

The jurisdiction of the Court of Special Appeals covers any reviewable judgment, decree, order, or other action of a circuit court. In addition, the court considers requests for appeals in areas such as post conviction, inmate grievances, and bail review. As Table 5-6 shows, the

Table 5-4. CIRCUIT COURT—FILINGS BY FISCAL YEAR

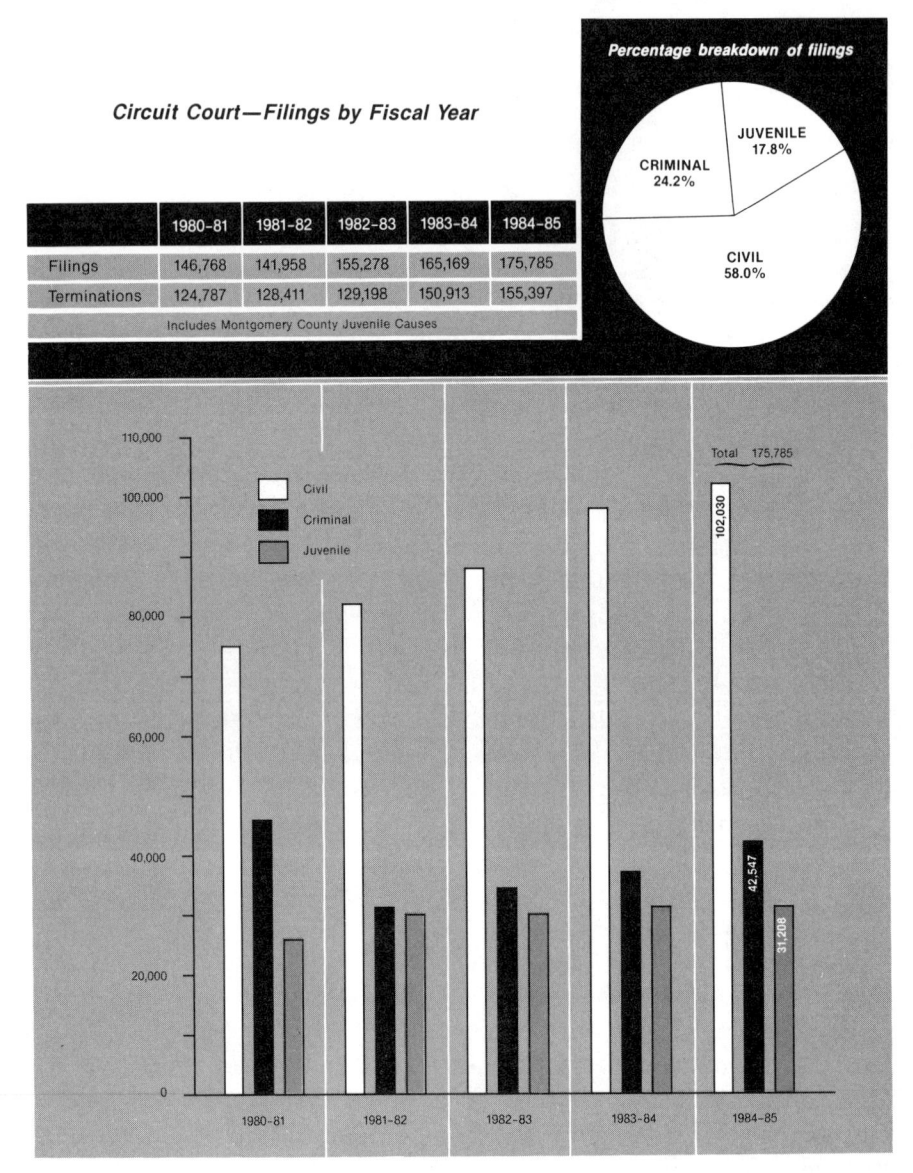

Circuit Court—Filings by Fiscal Year

	1980-81	1981-82	1982-83	1983-84	1984-85
Filings	146,768	141,958	155,278	165,169	175,785
Terminations	124,787	128,411	129,198	150,913	155,397

Includes Montgomery County Juvenile Causes

Percentage breakdown of filings
- JUVENILE 17.8%
- CRIMINAL 24.2%
- CIVIL 58.0%

1984-85 Total 175,785; Civil 102,030; Criminal 42,547; Juvenile 31,208

total number of cases brought to the Court of Special Appeals had steadily risen until 1982 and has declined slightly since then. The division between civil and criminal cases has fluctuated, but has been relatively equal.

The ability to appeal the decision of a court has generally been seen as an important element of the American system of justice. Appeals

Table 5-5. PERCENTAGES OF ORIGINAL CASES FILED AND REOPENED CASES FILED, JULY 1, 1984–JUNE 30, 1985, FISCAL 1985

	CIVIL		CRIMINAL		JUVENILE		TOTAL	
	Number	Percent	Number	Percent	Number	Percent	Number	Percent
FIRST CIRCUIT	4,244	66.7	1,594	25.0	528	8.3	6,366	100.0
Dorchester	1,071	72.4	260	17.6	149	10.0	1,480	100.0
Somerset	562	74.0	155	20.4	42	5.6	759	100.0
Wicomico	1,425	63.5	632	28.2	188	8.3	2,245	100.0
Worcester	1,186	63.0	547	29.1	149	7.9	1,882	100.0
SECOND CIRCUIT	3,978	70.7	956	17.0	691	12.3	5,625	100.0
Caroline	673	75.0	142	15.8	82	9.2	897	100.0
Cecil	1,701	68.5	429	17.3	354	14.2	2,484	100.0
Kent	270	72.6	54	14.5	48	12.9	372	100.0
Queen Anne's	671	71.5	165	17.6	103	10.9	939	100.0
Talbot	663	71.1	166	17.8	104	11.1	933	100.0
THIRD CIRCUIT	14,168	56.3	7,136	28.4	3,840	15.3	25,144	100.0
Baltimore	11,200	55.5	5,799	28.7	3,177	15.8	20,176	100.0
Harford	2,968	59.7	1,337	26.9	663	13.4	4,968	100.0
FOURTH CIRCUIT	4,016	67.5	844	14.2	1,087	18.3	5,947	100.0
Allegany	1,048	61.6	248	14.6	406	23.8	1,702	100.0
Garrett	510	71.0	113	15.7	95	13.3	718	100.0
Washington	2,458	69.7	483	13.7	586	16.6	3,527	100.0
FIFTH CIRCUIT	16,743	64.3	5,135	19.7	4,159	16.0	26,037	100.0
Anne Arundel	12,645	69.3	2,562	14.0	3,043	16.7	18,250	100.0
Carroll	1,784	50.4	1,134	32.0	625	17.6	3,543	100.0
Howard	2,314	54.5	1,439	33.9	491	11.6	4,244	100.0
SIXTH CIRCUIT	13,838	59.0	5,465	23.3	4,169	17.7	23,472	100.0
Frederick	1,883	69.3	487	17.9	348	12.8	2,718	100.0
Montgomery*	11,955	57.6	4,978	24.0	3,821	18.4	20,754	100.0
SEVENTH CIRCUIT	21,695	60.2	7,987	22.1	6,384	17.7	36,066	100.0
Calvert	798	54.4	342	23.3	327	22.3	1,467	100.0
Charles	1,860	58.2	613	19.2	722	22.6	3,195	100.0
Prince George's	18,046	60.3	6,707	22.4	5,163	17.3	29,916	100.0
St. Mary's	991	66.6	325	21.8	172	11.6	1,488	100.0
EIGHTH CIRCUIT	23,348	49.5	13,430	28.5	10,350	22.0	47,128	100.0
Baltimore City	23,348	49.5	13,430	28.5	10,350	22.0	47,128	100.0
STATE	102,030	58.0	42,547	24.2	31,208	17.8	175,785	100.0

*Juvenile causes heard at District Court level.

are not, for the most part, automatically granted however. A major reform in the judicial system in the country, including in Maryland, has been to give appeals courts control over which cases they hear. Moreover, decisions of lower courts are more often affirmed than reversed. Table 5-7 shows the disposition of cases which reached the Maryland Court of Special Appeals in 1984–85 and reflects the general pattern.

Table 5-6. THE COURT OF SPECIAL APPEALS, APPEALS DOCKETED BY TERM, COURT OF SPECIAL APPEALS REGULAR DOCKET

Year	Total	Criminal	Civil
1974	1154	631	523
1975	1384	762	622
1976	1383	675	708
1977	1412	684	728
1978	1416	665	751
1979	1671	796	875
1980*	1722	820	902
1981*	1742	870	872
1982*	1968	1107	861
1983*	1777	927	850
1984*	1642	751	891

*Does not include civil notices of appeal which were filed in the Clerk's Office pursuant to Maryland Rules 1022–1024. These appeals were either scheduled for prehearing conference or proceeded through the regular appellate process as stipulated in Maryland Rule 1024a.1. Cases finally disposed of by prehearing conference are never placed on the regular docket or listed as filings. Cases not finally disposed of by this process will be placed on subsequent dockets and will then be included among filings.

COURT OF APPEALS

The highest court in Maryland is the Court of Appeals, which dates back to the state's first constitution of 1776. The Court is composed of seven members, one from each of the first five Appellate Judicial circuits and two from the Sixth Appellate Judicial Circuit (Baltimore City).

The primary source for cases are ones that have been decided by the Court of Special Appeals, although the Court of Appeals may bring up for review cases filed in that court before they are decided there. In addition, the Court of Appeals may review certain decisions directly from the circuit court level.

The Court of Appeals has almost total control over its docket as a result of legislation passed in 1975. Deciding which cases to take is a significant element of the Court's power as well as a major demand on its time. For example, the Court's dispositions for 1984–85 (see Table 5-8) included 678 petitions for review and 161 cases decided. Of those 678 requests, the Court agreed to hear 90 cases, or 13.1 percent.

Table 5-7. CASES DISPOSED BY COURT OF SPECIAL APPEALS, REGULAR DOCKET, JULY 1, 1984–JUNE 30, 1985, FISCAL 1985

	Civil	Juvenile	Criminal	Total
Affirmed	385	13	634	1,032
Reversed	139	7	67	213
Dismissed—Opinion Filed	33	0	4	37
Dismissed Without Opinion	3	0	0	3
Remanded Without Affirmance or Reversal	7	1	6	14
Affirmed in Part, Reversed in Part	65	1	51	117
Modified and Affirmed	4	0	0	4
Stayed	3	0	2	5
Dismissed Prior to Argument or Submission	209	11	98	318
Transferred to Court of Appeals	57	1	6	64
Origin[a]				
1983 Docket	100	6	141	247
1984 Docket	766	25	702	1,493
1985 Docket	39	3	25	67
Total Cases Disposed During Fiscal 1985	905	34	868	1,807

[a] Annual reports prior to fiscal 1983 combined under "origin" cases disposed and cases pending, excluding pending cases filed during the current docket year.

An overview of Court of Appeals decisions for the 161 cases is shown in Table 5-9. Well over half the cases were civil. With respect to decisions, the overall balance was about equal between civil and criminal cases affirmed or dismissed, and cases revised or remanded.

The Court of Appeals represents the final word on questions of state law and the Maryland Constitution.[3] The existence of the Court affords the opportunity for review of lower court decisions as well as for the interpretation of both state laws and the Maryland Constitution.

The Court of Appeals, in being selective in the cases that it takes, is attempting to concentrate on the most important issues facing the community. One recent example, discussed in Chapter 2, was the Court of Appeals interpretation of the Maryland Constitution's requirements

Table 5-8. DISPOSITION OF TOTAL CASELOAD, COURT OF APPEALS, JULY 1, 1984–JUNE 30, 1985, FISCAL 1985

Regular Docket	161
Petitions for Certiorari	678
Attorney Grievance Proceedings	34
Bar Admissions Proceedings	7
Certified Questions of Law	5
Miscellaneous Appeals	25
Total Dispositions	910

Table 5-8a. PETITION DOCKET DISPOSITIONS,* (PETITIONS FOR CERTIORARI), JULY 1, 1984–JUNE 30, 1985, FISCAL 1985

	Granted	Dismissed	Denied	Withdrawn	Total
PETITIONS	90	6	581	1	678
Civil	56	6	262	1	325
Criminal	34	0	319	0	353

*713 filed in fiscal year 1985.

Table 5-9. DISPOSITION OF COURT OF APPEALS CASES, REGULAR DOCKET, JULY 1, 1984–JUNE 30, 1985, FISCAL 1985

	Civil	Juvenile	Criminal	Total
Affirmed	32	1	32	65
Reversed	30	0	24	54
Dismissed—Opinion Filed	2	0	1	3
Dismissed Without Opinion	4	0	4	8
Remanded Without Affirmance or Reversal	2	0	1	3
Vacated and Remanded	10	0	1	11
Affirmed in Part, Reversed in Part	11	0	2	13
Dismissed Prior to Argument or Submission	3	0	0	3
Transferred to Court of Special Appeals	1	0	0	1
Rescinded	0	0	0	0
Origin				
1982 Docket	4	0	7	11
1983 Docket	38	0	23	61
1984 Docket	50	1	33	84
1985 Docket	3	0	2	5
Total Cases Disposed During Fiscal 1985	95	1	65	161

NOTE: Origin totals in annual reports prior to fiscal 1983 combined cases disposed during the fiscal year and cases pending from completed docket years. (See Note to Table CA-10.)

with respect to public education funding in Maryland. The constitutionality of the death penalty represents another area in which the court is required to deal with a controversial and complex issue.

A 1985 case is a good illustration of the widespread impact that Court of Appeals decisions can have, sometimes even going beyond the boundaries of Maryland. The Court in *Olen J. Kelly* v. *R. G. Industries* ruled that the manufacturer and sellers of a cheap handgun, the so-called "Saturday Night Special," might be liable for injuries resulting from its use.[4] Some observers have applauded the decision as a landmark one in the national debate over gun control while others are highly critical of the ruling.

"*Outrageous! This Court Ruling Means We Could Get Sued!*"

A Baltimore *Sun* political cartoon

The Court of Appeals has a number of additional functions beyond the review of cases. For one, the Court has the authority to adopt rules of judicial administration, practice, and procedure, which have the force of law within the court system of Maryland. The Administrative Office of the Courts, which is responsible to the Chief Judge of the Court of Appeals, provides information, advice, facilities, and staff to assist in the administrative functions of the court. The Court of Appeals also admits persons to the practice of law in Maryland, reviews recommendations of the State Board of Law Examiners, and conducts disciplinary proceedings involving attorneys.

The state judicial system is also governed by the U. S. Constitution, as was discussed in Chapter 2. Thus, on occasion, a case in the state

Saturday Night Specials

The Maryland Court of Appeals has ruled that manufacturers and marketers of "Saturday night specials" are liable for damages that criminals inflict on victims with these guns. This is a sensible decision that should reduce the availability of this preferred weapon of street criminals, and possibly crime itself.

The "Saturday night special" is precisely defined by the federal government on the basis of several features. The most critical of these is barrel length. A gun with a barrel of three inches or less can be easily concealed by the street hoodlum. Such guns, especially the cheaper sort like the German-made one in the case before the Court of Appeals, are only accurate to about two feet.

Some handgun apologists argue that these weapons are needed for self-defense in the home, but experts, including police, say they are less effective for that purpose than full-sized pistols, and probably less effective than shotguns and German shepherds.

According to the Department of Justice, three-fourths of all gun murders and assaults and 90 percent of all gun robberies involve handguns. In those cases, the preferred gun is the short-barreled handgun. A recent study of 14,286 guns seized in street crimes showed that one in seven were cheap models that, like the one in the Maryland case, were made by the Roehm firm in Germany or assembled by a plant in Florida using Roehm parts. If manufacturers quit making and merchants quit selling these guns out of fear of being sued for damages, the criminal arsenal will be substantially reduced.

But that won't be enough. *Most* guns used in street crimes are well-made, expensive short-barreled handguns that do not meet the "Saturday night special" definition, though they are just as concealable and just as unsuited for purposes other than hurting and killing people at close range. Smith & Wesson made more of the seized crime guns in the study than Roehm.

The Court of Appeals has taken a step toward abolishing "Saturday night specials." We hope the next victim will be the expensive short-barreled handguns that are just as dangerous.

A Baltimore *Sun* editorial

---

court system, which raises federal constitutional issues, may be appealed to the U. S. Supreme Court. In addition, the decisions of the U. S. Supreme Court on cases outside Maryland may affect the rulings and interpretations of the Maryland courts on subsequent decisions.

SELECTION OF JUDGES

The selection of judges is an essential aspect of the Maryland judicial system. Article IV of the Maryland Constitution describes the selection of judges, their terms of office, the removal procedures, the different levels of the court system, and the selection and operation of court officials.

In the Court of Appeals, judges are initially appointed by the governor with confirmation by the Senate. The appointees then run for office without opposition at the next general election. If the judge does not win voter approval, the office becomes vacant. Judges serve ten-year terms. The Chief Judge of the Court of Appeals is designated by the governor.

Judges in the Court of Special Appeals are initially appointed by the governor with confirmation of the Senate. They also run on their records without opposition. The ten-year term of office to which these judges are elected is identical to the process in the Court of Appeals. The chief judge is selected by the governor.

The selection of Circuit Court judges is distinct from the other two higher courts. Each circuit judge is initially appointed to office by the governor and then must run for a fifteen-year term at the next regularly scheduled general election. The appointee may be opposed by any qualified member of the bar in the election.

In the District Court, judges are appointed by the governor with confirmation of the Senate. These judges serve ten-year terms and do not run for election.

The issue of judges running for office in elections has been a controversial one. On the one hand, proposals to remove judges from the election process have been made on the grounds that the office is and should be nonpolitical, and that the public may not have the means to evaluate the performance of judges. The other position on this issue is that the public should have the opportunity to remove judges from office if they are not performing adequately. In the same vein some supporters of the current system contend that the initial selection process excludes many competent and qualified prospects, who would have a chance through the election process.

Other Participants in the Judicial System

The workings of the judicial system involve more than just judges. The laws that courts interpret and apply are passed by the legislature and may be changed. The enforcement of judicial decisions is the responsibility of the executive branch of government. There are, moreover, many other participants in court cases in addition to judges.

In the first place, there are parties to a law case. One party, called the plaintiff, initiates the case, in essence asking the court to take a particular action. In a criminal case, the plaintiff is the State of Maryland or one of the political jurisdictions, which is alleging that a criminal law has been violated. In a civil case, the plaintiff is an individual, or corporation, who is requesting a remedy from the courts, whether it be monetary compensation for some kind of damages, or an order to perform an act, or an injunction to stop something from being done.

> **Question:** Under current Maryland law, Circuit Court judges must run in competitive elections, immediately following their appointment to the bench. A Maryland Bar Association Task Force has proposed a constitutional amendment which would substitute a Merit Retention System in place of the current election system.
>
> Under the Merit Retention System, judges would run in non-partisan merit retention elections, in which other candidates would not challenge the judge. Rather, voters would decide only whether to retain or reject the individual judge, not whether to replace him with another candidate.
>
> Those who favor the change feel it will reduce political influence, and encourage qualified individuals to seek judicial appointments. Opponents feel it will only increase the influence of the bar, and limit the number of minorities and women appointed to the bench.
>
> | FAVOR | OPPOSE | UNDECIDED |
> |---|---|---|
> | 40% | 29% | 31% |
>
> Source: Mason-Dixon Opinion Research, Inc., Columbia, Maryland. Maryland Opinion Poll, November 1983.

The other party to a case is the defendant. In a criminal case, the defendant is a person who has been charged with a crime. In a civil case, the defendant is the person being sued.

In most instances, both the plaintiff and the defendant are represented by lawyers. Depending on the type of case, the lawyer may be an attorney in private practice or a member of one of several agencies or organizations that are part of the state judicial system.

Prosecution of criminal cases is carried out by the Office of the State's Attorney, an elected position in each county and in Baltimore City. The State's Attorney, who serves a four-year term, has a staff of lawyers who assist in the work of the office. State's attorneys have considerable discretion in which cases they will prosecute, which cases they will drop or settle, and what areas of crime they will emphasize.

Defendants in criminal cases are represented by a lawyer they choose if they can afford the expense. Alternatively, defendants without adequate financial resources may have access to the services of the Office of the Public Defender. This office, which is funded by the state, provides free legal services to indigent defendants. The existence of a public defender system in Maryland is a direct result of a U. S. Supreme Court ruling that the Sixth Amendment to the Constitution guarantees everyone the right to an attorney, regardless of his or her financial condition.[5]

In civil cases, there is also a mechanism to provide legal services for persons with limited incomes. The Maryland Legal Services Corporation has a number of Legal Aid Bureaus around the state which provide free legal assistance to individuals who meet certain income qualifications. Legal Aid may represent either plaintiffs or defendants in legal disputes. In addition, some private law firms provide free, or *pro bono*, legal assistance to needy clients on a limited basis.

Finally, there is the State Law Department, which is headed by the Attorney General. The attorney general's position is an elected one, for a four-year term. The attorney general is responsible for representing the state in all appellate court cases, for serving as legal adviser to all state departments, agencies, boards, and commissions, for giving legal opinions on a number of questions, and for prosecuting violators in some areas of state law. For example, the attorney general's office conducted an investigation which led to indictments in the 1985 savings and loan scandal.

The Courts and the Political System

The courts are, in most respects, passive. They wait for cases to be brought to them. Judges are bound by rules and precedents in the actions they take. Moreover, the courts are dependent on others to carry out or enforce their decisions. All of these factors can be seen as restraints or limits on the power of courts.[6]

Nevertheless, the courts are an important and influential institution in our system of government. They are often involved in issues of great controversy and may, at times, be the subject of intense criticism.

Whether judges interpret the law or rule on the basis of their own policy preferences is a matter of constant debate.[7] While these discussions most often focus on patterns of decision making at the federal level, the actions of individual judges at the state and local level can be of great significance as well.

For example, in Boston, Massachusetts, Judge Arthur Garrity in effect ran the city school system for a number of years as a means of implementing a desegregation order.[8] In Maryland, Judge Joseph Kaplan exercised considerable authority and discretion in overseeing the legal disposition of the savings and loan scandal of 1985.

Difficult issues often end up in the courts. Whether or not there are legal solutions, the involving of the courts shows the connection between the different branches of government. Similarly, the courts are sometimes blamed for problems that the other branches of the government are struggling to deal with.

There are numerous examples of these interrelationships. The problem of crime is one of the most serious in our society today. Public opinion polls regularly show that people are more concerned about crime than about any other single issue. Debates about ways to reduce crime and to improve law enforcement often center on the role of the courts.

A few examples can make this point. By far the most controversial issue has been the insistence by courts on the maintenance of strict procedures in the investigation and prosecution of persons accused of crimes.[9] A series of United States Supreme Court decisions in the 1960s, which were also binding on Maryland Courts, required that a set of clear protections be afforded anyone accused of a crime. The result, in the minds of some observers, is that individuals have, on occasion, been released on "technicalities" when they were actually guilty. The response has been that our constitutional system assumes a person to be innocent until proven guilty and that it guarantees all individuals certain rights to protect them in the judicial process.

Critics of this latter approach go further however. They suggest that strict interpretation of defendants' rights hampers police law enforcement efforts and actually may increase crime. There has, in fact, been something of a drawing back by the courts in their interpretation of procedural rights of persons accused of crimes. Whatever the actual effect on crime, the procedures used in criminal cases have been the subject of ongoing controversy and of some modification and adjustment.

There are other controversial issues involving the courts. A movement that has developed in recent years has stressed the importance of victims' rights in the judicial process. The sentencing practices of judges have drawn considerable attention, with respect to both consistency and to particular crimes such as drunk driving. The practice of plea bargaining, which reduces the backlog of the court's docket but may allow less severe punishments than some observers think are justified, has also been criticized.

The step after the courts in the criminal justice process has also been widely debated in recent years. The effect of imprisonment, the conditions within prisons, and the need for additional correctional facilities have all been subjects of constant discussion, although not consensus or resolution. There are numerous paradoxes in the debate about prisons. On the one hand, there seems to be considerable support for longer prison sentences for convicted criminals. On the other, there is little enthusiasm for spending scarce public resources for prison facilities. Moreover, there is little or no support for locating prisons in any particular area. Even people who agree that more prisons are needed think that they should be placed "somewhere else."

Conclusion

The judicial system is an integral part of our system of government. Most people are less familiar with the courts than with the other branches of government because they do not come into direct contact with them. Yet the workings of the judicial system have a significant effect on our lives even if there is no direct contact. Moreover, when and if we are involved with the courts, the consequences may be very significant.

The courts are not generally seen as political in nature, but in fact they are a key element of our overall political system and are interrelated with the other portions of our government. The different branches affect each other and respond to the other's actions. The workings of the judicial system may be less well known, but they are not less important.

Chapter 6

THE ADMINISTRATION OF STATE GOVERNMENT: BUREAUCRATS AND BUREAUCRACY

Elected officials of state government receive the most attention from the press and the public, but the portion of the state government that citizens are most likely to have direct contact with is the state bureaucracy. We receive many valuable services as a result of these contacts, but the image of bureaucrats and of bureaucracy is not always a positive one. Critics speak of red tape, waste, and inefficiency. Bureaucracy is seen by some observers as unresponsive and insensitive.[1] While evidence of these defects can be found, it is not completely clear that they are problems unique to the public sector. The same difficulties can be encountered in private organizations as well. At the same time, professionalism and a real commitment to service are also found in public bureaucracies.[2]

Much of the controversy about bureaucracy results not from *how* the work is done, but, instead, from *what* is done. Opponents of particular programs, who failed to convince the legislature of their position, may shift their attention to the implementation of the program and to the bureaucracy. Some state programs provide benefits to a limited and identifiable segment of the population, whether by geography, income level, or some other factor. People not in those groups or not needing the particular services may oppose spending their tax dollars on the activity.

Neither the complaints about bureaucracy nor the criticism of its activities is going to end. Controversy about implementation will occur wherever there is significant disagreement about the goals of a particular program. Similarly, the efforts to improve the management of organizations, whether public or private, will continue.

With this overall context in mind, we can look at the principal characteristics of the state bureaucracy in Maryland, including public employees, the agencies and departments of state government, and the main activities in which they engage.

Bureaucrats

Government is the largest employer in the state of Maryland. The total number of state employees is over 90,000 which rates Maryland eighteenth in the United States, the same ranking as the state's overall population. Another 160,000 persons work for local government, while approximately 256,000 state residents work for the federal government.[3]

According to the State Department of Personnel, the "average state employee" is "39 years old, has ten years of service, and earns $17,700 yearly."[4] This description does not show the diversity of the state workforce. Table 6-1 provides additional details for full-time employees. The range of salaries for state civil servants is shown in Table 6-2.

A major characteristic of government employment is the use of the merit system.[5] In contrast to the spoils systems of the nineteenth century, where continued government employment was determined by the results of each election, the merit system establishes a permanent, career civil service. Initial eligibility is determined by qualifying on a test or by specific experience and education criteria. Civil servants cannot be fired if they are doing their jobs adequately, and they are promoted on the basis of job performance.

Under the merit system, the State of Maryland pledges equality in employment, job classification, and promotions. State employees who feel they have been discriminated against because of race, religion, national origin, sex, or age may file a complaint with the Secretary of Personnel or with the Maryland Commission on Human Relations. Each state job is classified according to designated responsibilities and duties performed, with those jobs with similar functions being given the same classification and salary range. Although most employees enter state service through competitive examination, certain staff and administrative jobs are filled by the secretary of the department. Unlike merit system employees, these appointees can be removed from their jobs at any time and do not have the right to file a grievance or appeal.

Some critics have argued that there are insufficient incentives within the civil service system because it is so difficult to fire employees, and that this is a major cause of unresponsiveness within the bureauc-

Table 6-1. STATE GOVERNMENT EMPLOYEES

Job Categories	Total	Male	% Male	All Employees Female	% Female	Total Min.	% Min.
A. Officials/Administrators	1,660	1,355	81.6	305	18.3	193	11.6
B. Professionals	16,652	8,980	53.9	7,672	46.0	3,710	22.2
C. Technicians	4,334	2,552	58.8	1,782	41.1	927	21.3
D. Protective Service Workers	5,809	5,106	87.8	703	12.1	2,167	37.3
E. Paraprofessionals	6,990	1,607	22.9	5,383	77.0	3,765	53.8
F. Office/Clerical	12,066	1,336	11.0	10,730	88.9	3,773	31.2
G. Skilled Craft Workers	1,532	1,479	96.5	53	3.4	272	17.7
H. Service Maintenance	5,184	3,544	68.3	1,640	31.6	2,105	40.6
TOTAL	54,227	25,959	47.8	28,268	52.1	16,912	31.1

Source: Department of Personnel, State of Maryland, *Annual Report, 1984*.

Table 6-2. STANDARD SALARY SCHEDULE, FISCAL YEAR 1987

Grade	Base	Step 1	Step 2	Step 3	Step 4	Step 5	Step 6
1	9,520	9,956	10,427	10,986	11,585	11,797	12,026
2	10,037	10,502	11,034	11,632	12,296	12,536	12,779
3	10,609	11,114	11,682	12,351	13,068	13,321	13,581
4	11,256	11,821	12,460	13,183	13,951	14,219	14,499
5	11,972	12,620	13,316	14,091	14,922	15,221	15,527
6	12,782	13,479	14,231	15,079	15,981	16,301	16,629
7	13,619	14,363	15,186	16,098	17,065	17,406	17,754
8	14,513	15,336	16,240	17,215	18,249	18,612	18,986
9	15,568	16,456	17,445	18,493	19,600	19,993	20,392
10	16,734	17,710	18,772	19,897	21,094	21,514	21,949
11	18,014	19,077	20,221	21,436	22,723	23,179	23,642
12	19,392	20,547	21,782	23,086	24,473	24,965	25,464
13	20,886	22,134	23,463	24,873	26,365	26,893	27,430
14	22,493	23,845	25,274	26,795	28,402	28,971	29,552
15	24,233	25,685	27,225	28,858	30,592	31,205	31,828
16	26,110	27,676	29,338	31,098	32,964	33,625	34,295
17	28,199	29,889	31,684	33,586	35,599	36,315	37,040
18	30,452	32,279	34,219	36,270	38,447	39,217	40,002
19	32,889	34,862	36,957	39,173	41,526	42,357	43,202
20	35,522	37,652	39,908	42,307	44,845	45,744	46,659
21	38,365	40,666	43,105	45,693	48,434	49,405	50,393
22	41,051	43,513	46,123	48,892	51,825	52,864	53,921

Source: Department of Personnel, State of Maryland, *The Marylander*, Summer 1986.

racy. Reforms that link promotions and raises to evaluations of productivity are one response to these criticisms. Another is the creation of "unclassified positions," that is, political appointments which are not subject to the same job security as civil service positions.

Another approach to improving the quality of public employees is the movement toward professionalism within the civil service. Examples include enrollment by public employees in graduate degree programs, particularly in public administration, provision of on-the-job development and training programs, and the adoption of evaluation systems based on productivity. A variety of advanced degree programs are offered at state universities, while the Department of Personnel through its Management Development Center provides specific training programs.

A significant element of public employment today is unionization. Major public employee unions in Maryland include the Maryland Clas-

State employees' salaries lag behind national average

United Press International

BALTIMORE — A federal census report released Wednesday showed Maryland state employees' salaries lag far behind the national average.

As of October 1984, the U.S. Census Bureau ranked Maryland salaries 27th out of 50 states. The average monthly income for full-time state employees was $1,638, while the national average was $1,744.

Joseph Adler, executive director of the Maryland Classified Employees Association said figures were dismal.

"This is an outrage! Last year Maryland ranked 25th; this year we rank 27th. We are going backwards at a time when all responsible people have realized and have stated that Maryland's salaries need to be brought up to a much higher level," he said in a prepared statement.

Neighboring mid-Atlantic states also ranked below the national average, according to the census report. Virginia's monthly average in 1984 was $1,513, Delaware ranked 34th with $1,521 per month, and Pennsylvania was listed as $1,699.

Top state salaries in 1984 were earned in Alaska and California with $2,230 and $2,156 respectively. Mississippi was at the very bottom of the list with $1,168 per month.

Maryland state employees in the non-teaching educational field ranked 48th out of 50, according to the report. Maryland's salaries were $1,189 while the national average was estimated at $1,609 per month.

"The salaries of these employees are abysmally low. We are only two from the bottom. Obviously, the state needs to do much more and to spend the necessary resources to bring everyone up to par," Adler said.

"We implore the governor and the legislature to commit the resources and significantly elevate the salaries of all state employees," he said.

Michael Glass, of Maryland's state personnel office, said the figures surprise him, and though he was aware state salaries are low he said, "We don't really compare salaries nationally."

The census report indicated a positive overall note for Maryland, however.

Statistics show the state's personal per capita income ranked 7th out of 50 states. Maryland's per capita income for all residents was $14,111 while the national average rested at $12,207.

"The bottom line is that Maryland ranks above the national average in terms of per capita income, but ranks below the 50th percentile for compensating its employees. This situation needs to be remedied if the state wants a productive and efficient work force," Adler said.

---

sified Employees Association (MCEA), the American Federation of State, County, and Municipal Employees (AFSCME), and various specialized occupational groups such as teachers, fire fighters, and police. At state and local levels, approximately fifty percent of government employees belong to a union.

It is sometimes argued that unionization is fundamentally incompatible with the concept of public service.[6] The specific focus of this debate generally centers on whether public unions have the right to strike. Many states specifically forbid strikes by public employees, although some have occurred anyway. At the state and local level, the most frequent instances have been strikes by public school teachers.

In Maryland, there are a variety of different laws governing collective bargaining, differing by jurisdictions and government functions. Proposals to create a uniform collective bargaining system for the entire state have not been adopted, but continue to be discussed.

Maryland's Bureaucracy

Maryland's state bureaucracy contains fourteen executive departments, approximately ninety independent agencies, and numerous boards and commissions, some of which are permanent while others are temporary. Each of these organizations has specific responsibilities assigned to it, although there may be overlap and the specific roles may change over time.

The organization of state government, the middle level of the federal system, is affected by the activities which are undertaken at the national and the local levels. A major current federal initiative may result in the creation of a new state agency to carry out the program. Similarly, the decision to transfer a governmental function from the local to the state level could also result in reorganization of state government.

The public's view of the role of government and the kinds of activities that are seen as necessary and appropriate will also affect the structure of state government. The relatively recent concern in the United States with environmental matters led to the creation of the Federal Environmental Protection Agency and to a greater environmental focus within both the state's Department of Natural Resources and the Department of Health and Mental Hygiene.

Attention to efficiency and effectiveness may also lead to government reorganization. Agencies are generally established one at a time. There is not always an effort made to consider and relate the activities of one agency to another, with the result that there may be overlap and duplication. In Maryland, by the late 1960s, there were nearly two hundred and fifty governmental organizations of one kind or the other. A series of bills passed by the General Assembly between 1969 and 1972 consolidated most of those agencies into twelve major departments, with an existing department designated as executive level in 1976 and a new cabinet department established in 1983.

Each department is headed by a secretary appointed by the governor with the advice and confirmation of the Senate. The secretaries serve at the pleasure of and report directly to the governor. Secretaries are responsible for carrying out the governor's policies concerning their departments, for the operation of their departments, and for establishing the guidelines and procedures for the orderly and efficient administration of their departments.

With the approval of the governor, the secretary appoints a deputy secretary who has duties provided by law or delegated by the secretary. The deputy secretary, along with the staff assistants and professional consultants, serve at the pleasure of the secretary. Other employees in the department are under the state merit system. Table 6-3 shows executive, or cabinet level, departments.

THE ADMINISTRATION OF STATE GOVERNMENT

Governor Schaefer meets with his executive committee.

The major executive departments can be divided into two distinct categories. The first are those departments that are responsible for the functioning of government directly. These activities, which include financing, staffing, and planning, are referred to as *staff* functions. Four specific departments in this category warrant a brief description.

Table 6-3. MARYLAND GOVERNMENT EXECUTIVE DEPARTMENTS

Department	Number of Positions	Budget (1985)
Agriculture	514	$ 27,309,317
Budget and Fiscal Planning	111	5,056,043
Economic and Community Development	545	64,522,659
Education	1,362	1,520,196,391
Employment and Training	1,428	102,721,552
General Services	64	2,712,003
Health and Mental Hygiene	13,396	1,417,696,253
Human Resources	6,476	573,570,373
Licensing and Registration	633	26,716,054
Natural Resources	1,634	126,572,763
Personnel	40	2,954,842
Public Safety and Correctional Services	8,109	397,954,127
State Planning	99	4,178,348
Transportation	9,360	1,410,643,469

Source: General Assembly of Maryland, *The Maryland State Budget for the Fiscal Year Ending June 30. 1986.*

The *Department of Budget and Fiscal Planning*, in its present form, was established in 1969, but dates back to 1916. The primary activity of the department is to develop the governor's budget each year. Through this process, the department is directly involved in management and coordination of the activities of other state agencies. Related responsibilities include supervision of budget execution, revenue estimating, and coordination of state automatic data processing.

The *Department of General Services* is responsible for the functions which relate primarily to engineering, construction, and maintenance of state facilities, procurement of supplies and equipment, and maintenance of important state records. The department was created in 1970 and combined the functions of several state agencies. To understand the responsibilities of the Department of General Services, consider, for example, that the state owns or rents office space totaling almost 4 million square feet and annually purchases commodities ranging from office supplies to food products at a total dollar value of over $110 million.

A third support agency is the *Department of Personnel*. Its task of administering the state personnel system includes recruitment and placement of employees; establishment and maintenance of salary and wage plans; development of training programs; and supervision of the

THE ADMINISTRATION OF STATE GOVERNMENT 105

The Evening Sun

BALTIMORE, WEDNESDAY, JANUARY 15, 1986

Briefing reporters yesterday on the proposed state budget for 1987 are, from left, Comptroller Louis Goldstein, budget secretary Louis Stettler, Gov. Harry Hughes and Benjamin Bialek, the governor's chief legislative officer.

By Barbara Haddock—Evening Sun Staff

$38 million earmarked for housing

By Dan Fesperman
Evening Sun Staff

From the rundown brick rowhouses of Baltimore's bleakest slums to the flimsiest tar-paper shacks in the mountains and on the Eastern Shore, Marylanders living in substandard housing got a $38.8 million glimmer of hope today.

The hope came in the form of housing initiatives in the fiscal 1987 budget presented to the General Assembly by Gov. Harry R. Hughes. But clouding the hope somewhat was the prospect that a large amount of that money might not be so easy to get next year.

Hughes, in proposing the initiatives, embraced most of the key recommendations made last year by the Maryland Housing Policy Commission.

The initiatives include programs for assistance to low-income renters, abatement of lead-paint poisoning, housing rehabilitation, shared housing, low-interest mortgages

See HOUSING, A6, Col. 1

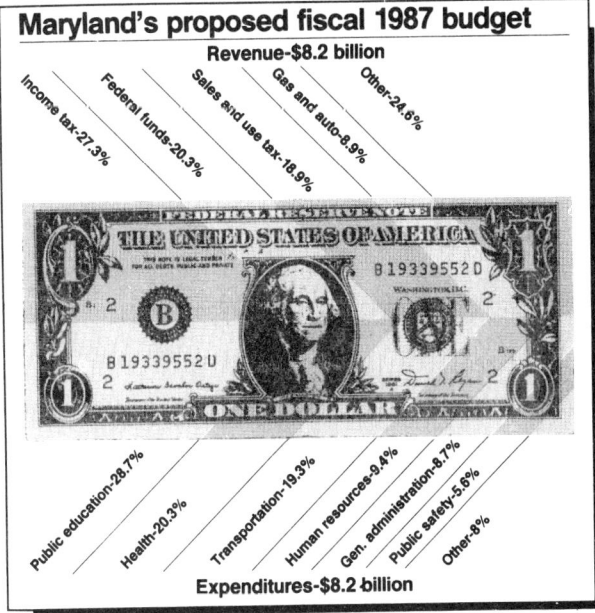

Maryland's proposed fiscal 1987 budget

Revenue—$8.2 billion

Income tax-27.3% / Federal funds-20.3% / Sales and use tax-18.9% / Gas and auto-8.9% / Other-24.6%

Public education-28.7% / Health-20.3% / Transportation-19.3% / Human resources-9.4% / Gen. administration-8.7% / Public safety-5.6% / Other-8%

Expenditures—$8.2 billion

The Evening Sun

state's labor relations policy. The Department of Personnel was established in 1970 as part of a series of governmental reorganizations. Marylanders other than state employees are most likely to come in contact with the Department of Personnel if they are applying for a state position, usually in the form of a competitive examination.

The fourth cabinet-level staff department is the *Department of State Planning*, which in its present form dates back to 1969. The department works with other state agencies on information and plans relevant to the future direction of state government, and is concerned with planning for overall state growth and development. The functions of greatest importance are the department's preparation of both the annual capital budget and the five year capital improvement program.

All four of these departments, as well as several additional independent agencies including the Maryland State Retirement Agency and the State Archives, are concerned with the maintenance and operation of state government. Their function is to allow the other departments of state government to provide the services that they are responsible for. We can now look at those other agencies.

The remaining ten cabinet-level agencies are responsible for the delivery of a variety of services to the citizens of Maryland. Sometime these departments are categorized into those that provide services directly to individuals and those whose activities are more general and whose benefits are indirect to most citizens. The former group is generally referred to as social service and human resources agencies, while the latter falls under the broad heading of economic development and environmental protection.

In fact, the range of activities of each of these departments makes this distinction one that is not always applicable. For example, the Department of Health and Mental Hygiene, which is primarily concerned with service delivery to individuals, has an Office of Environmental Health. The brief descriptions of those departments which follow will be supplemented by a general discussion of the major functions of state government.

The *Department of Agriculture* has the broad mandate of protecting and developing the agriculture interests of Maryland. The department, which includes a number of boards, commissions, and specialized agencies, is involved in inspection, disease prevention, and promotion of agriculture. This is an example of a department whose focus is on a particular group of people and a specific segment of the economy, the

THE ADMINISTRATION OF STATE GOVERNMENT

PUBLIC HEALTH ENGINEER III (0177)
(Maximum reached in six years)
$25,227 - $33,135
(Effective 7/1/85)

WORK FOR MARYLAND STATE GOVERNMENT

MINIMUM QUALIFICATIONS:
Education: Possession of a bachelor's degree from an accredited college or university in the field of engineering.
Experience: Two years of professional engineering experience in a field related to public health or environmental regulation.
Notes: 1. Pertinent volunteer and/or part-time experience is acceptable. Please document the number of hours spent per week in this type of experience on the application form (MS 100).
2. Applicants may substitute 30 semester credits of graduate education in the fields of engineering or public health from an accredited college or university for up to one year of required experience.
3. Registration as a Professional Engineer in the State of Maryland may be substituted for the required education.

CONDITIONS OF EMPLOYMENT:
1. Candidates may be given a medical examination to determine their ability to perform job related functions.

NATURE OF WORK:
This is highly responsible professional work as an engineering specialist in the State's environmental health services programs. The employee in this class is responsible for developing, implementing and evaluating comprehensive environmental health services programs including, but not limited to, sanitary engineering, industrial hygiene, air pollution, sanitation, and environmental safety.

IMPORTANT INFORMATION ABOUT EXAMINATION AND APPOINTMENT:
Applications will only be accepted for positions currently on the Department of Personnel's test schedule. For classifications not scheduled, applicants will need to have their names and addresses placed in an "INTEREST FILE" for positions of interest. This can be done by calling the Application Control Unit of the Department of Personnel, 383-2470 or toll free (within Maryland) at 1-800-492-7845. As examinations are announced, applicants will be mailed a post card advising them to file their applications by the closing date. Applications must be complete and accurate as they are part of the examination process.
Most examinations are written, oral and/or demonstration of a skill. Some examinations may be a rating of your qualifications as submitted on your application, and your score will depend on the completeness of that information. Promotional State employees receive seniority credits. Candidates are interviewed and work records are reviewed by hiring agency staff before selection. Special test arrangements and accommodations are made for handicapped candidates, providing the Department of Personnel is notified IN ADVANCE of the type and extent of the handicap. Attach a statement to your application requesting special assistance, if necessary. "STATE OF MARYLAND - AN EQUAL OPPORTUNITY EMPLOYER."

Date Adopted: July 1, 1980

DEPARTMENT OF PERSONNEL • State Office Building • 301 W. Preston St. • Baltimore, Maryland 21201

MS 120A

AN EQUAL OPPORTUNITY EMPLOYER

A job notice for employment with Maryland government

18,000 farms in Maryland. As a result, relatively few people in Maryland come into direct contact with the Department of Agriculture.

The focus of the *Department of Economic and Community Development* is much more general and also more widespread. Created in 1970, it is responsible for more than twenty programs divided into two broad areas: economic development, including financing and marketing; and housing and community development. Activities range from loan programs for multifamily housing to a Motion Picture and Television Development Office, which has assisted in the filming of several motion pictures in Maryland. The department is responsible for administering federal funds for housing rental subsidies and also generates revenues through its own activities, such as the Maryland Housing Fund, which provides insurance for both single family and multifamily mortgage loans.

Among the largest agencies of state government is the *Department of Health and Mental Hygiene*. The department's major roles are to meet health needs which are not provided by the private health care system; to perform health planning; and to set standards for improved health service delivery in Maryland. The largest program is Medical Assistance, a federally aided program that provides payments for medical care for certain low income persons. The organizational chart below illustrates the wide range of services provided by the Department of Health and Mental Hygiene.

The newest executive agency of Maryland government is the *Department of Employment and Training*, which was established in 1983. The department consolidates the principal employment and training programs of the state, which were previously scattered through a number of agencies. A large portion of the department's budget comes from the federal government supporting such major programs as Unemployment Insurance and Job Training.

In contrast to several of the preceding departments, the *Department of Natural Resources* is relatively small. Its activities involve planning, and coordinating and preserving the state's natural resources. The department's responsibilities include the state's forty-nine parks, ten state forests, thirty-six wildlife management areas, and a wide range of environmental concerns.

An agency that does receive a lot of attention is the *Department of Public Safety and Correctional Services*. While much of the public safety function is carried out by local police forces, this department's responsibilities are still important. The two divisions that are most prominent

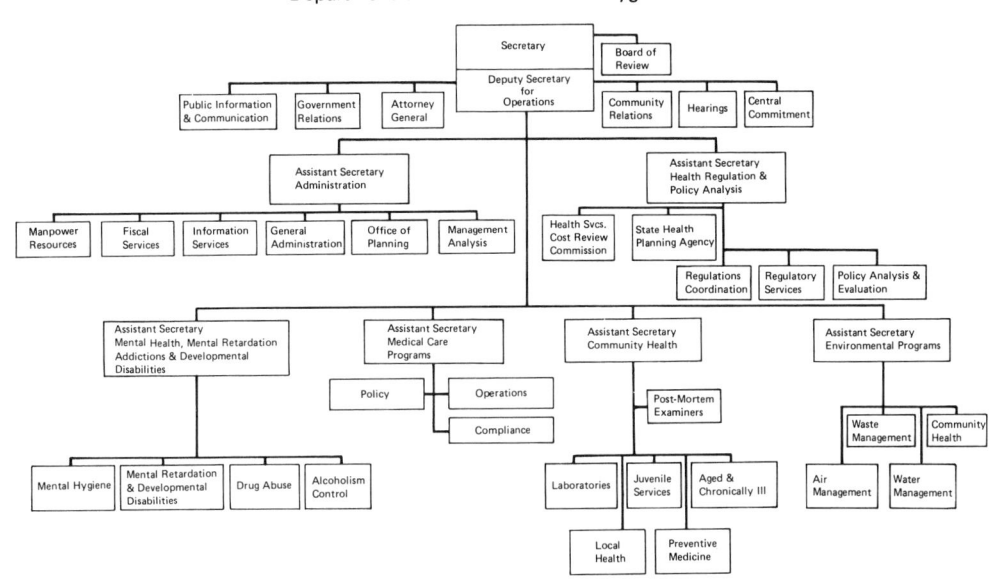

Department of Health and Mental Hygiene

are Corrections, which runs the state's prison system, and the Maryland State Police, which is responsible for enforcement of state traffic and criminal laws.

The *Department of Transportation* brings together a number of diverse activities in a single agency. Responsibilities of this department include highways, mass transit, the Port of Baltimore, motor vehicle administration, and Baltimore-Washington International Airport. The department is involved in direct services to citizens, such as licensing of drivers and motor vehicles, capital construction programs, including highways and the subway systems in both Baltimore and the Maryland suburbs of Washington, and maintenance of toll facilities.

The *Department of Licensing and Regulation* was created in 1970 to bring together many of the state's business regulation and occupational licensing programs. Specific regulatory divisions include: insurance, banking, occupational safety and health, and horse racing. There are, currently, twelve boards responsible for various licensing reviews, including most of the state nonmedical professionals.

The last cabinet-level agency is the *State Department of Education*, which dates back to 1870, but was designated as a principal department in 1976. Education is the single largest expenditure of state and local government in the United States, and Maryland is no exception to this pattern. The State Department of Education has overall responsibility for elementary and secondary education in Maryland. Basic standards and guidelines are established by this department, but the direct provision of education is the responsibility of the individual boards of education in each of the state's twenty-four political subdivisions. (See the discussion on education in Chapter 2.) The state distributes close to one billion dollars in various forms of aid to the local school systems.

Higher education in Maryland is not under the administrative control of a single department, but is nevertheless an important state activity. There are fifty-seven institutions of higher education in Maryland, thirty-two of which are public. The State Board for Higher Education, established in 1976, has a broad coordinating role, but does not directly run the different colleges and universities. The state provides nearly $390 million in state tax revenues to support higher education in Maryland.

The activities of state government are not confined to the departments which have been described in this section. In addition to the executive departments, there are close to one hundred boards, commissions, task forces and advisory boards. Some, like the Special Advisory Commission on Professional Sports and the Economy, receive a great deal of notice, while the activities of others such as the Governor's Task Force on Time-Sharing probably do not draw the attention of many citizens. For the most part, these various groups meet to study and make recommendations on a specific problem and then go out of existence.

There are also approximately ninety independent agencies of state government which do not have cabinet status but which may perform important tasks. All of the agencies concerned with higher education fall into this category, as do such agencies as the State Lottery, the Public Service Commission, the State Board of Election Laws, and the State Department of Assessments and Taxation.

Finally, there are another fourteen interstate agencies, in which Maryland officials work with representatives of other states on common problems and concerns. Examples include the Chesapeake Bay Commission and the Washington Metropolitan Area Transit Authority.

An Overview of the State Bureaucracy

The shape and size of Maryland's bureaucracy is constantly changing. The governor has extensive reorganization powers under the state constitution. The use of temporary organizations—commissions and task forces—is increasing in frequency. The relationship between

Citizen advisory committees work with state agencies.

the three layers of the federal system—national, state, and local—is always being reexamined and adjusted.

Moreover, as the previous section indicates, the scope and expenditures of state governmental activities vary enormously. The amount of public attention also differs significantly. An additional look at the three departments with the highest levels of expenditures shows more fully the impact of state government on the citizens of Maryland.

Three functional areas dwarf all the others, yet for very different reasons. Education has long been considered an essential public service. There is even, as was discussed in Chapter 2, a specific article in the Maryland Constitution that refers to the state's obligation to provide public schools. Moreover, most of the money spent on education comes from state and local sources. The federal government's contribution has never been a large one (see Table 6-4).

The level of public funding for education and the way in which that money is to be distributed are matters of recurrent debate. Maryland has had numerous special commissions in the past few years which have studied and made recommendations on this subject.[7] It has been the

Table 6-4. SOURCE OF CURRENT FUNDS, MARYLAND PUBLIC SCHOOLS: SCHOOL YEARS 1983–84 AND 1981–82

Income Source[a]	1983–84 Amount ($)	1981–82 Amount ($)	Percent of Total 1983–84	Percent of Total 1981–82
Federal Funds	135,602,964	133,309,309	6.7	7.1
State Funds	630,565,052	597,776,230	31.0	32.0
Local Funds	1,265,472,139	1,136,044,450	62.2	60.8

Source: Maryland Department of Economic and Community Development, *Maryland Statistical Abstract 1986–87*.

[a] Includes revenue for purchase of replacement and additional equipment for current expense purposes, and federal and state funds for food service programs. Excludes teachers' retirement and social security paid direct by state.

central focus of the General Assembly in some years; for example, in 1984 when legislators debated and voted on a series of proposals recommended by the Civiletti Commission to increase the amount of state aid to local school systems. The general population has demonstrated an ongoing concern about the quality of the public school system and has been more politically active on education issues than on most other public questions.

There is no reason to expect these patterns to change. The cost of public education is high, but we have long ago concluded that it is an essential public service. What we have not agreed on, and are unlikely to, is who should pay how much, and who should receive what portion. Ironically, much of the debate about education occurs at the local level. The state role has been primarily that of distributing funds to help support local school systems.

Second on the list of state departments, ranked by spending level, is the Department of Health and Mental Hygiene. The emphasis of this department's responsibilities is on direct services provided to specific individuals, based on certain eligibility criteria of need. The services are delivered, for the most part, at the local level and are often controversial. Health benefits, and other services such as those coming under human resources, tend to be seen by many as "redistributive," that is, resources taken away from one group, usually taxpayers, and given to another group, the program's beneficiaries.[8] Program goals and standards, eligibility criteria, and, indeed, the continuation of the programs at all, are subjects of continuing debate.

The third largest state expenditure is for transportation. A number of distinctions can be readily seen between this function and both education and health. Rather than providing a direct service to individuals, much of what the Department of Transportation does is to build, operate, and maintain capital structures that are available to the public as a whole. A good example is highway construction and maintenance, which cost approximately $300 million in 1984. The federal contribution to transportation activities is much greater than for education, accounting for over $500 million of the department's total expenditures in 1984, for example.

By contrast to these three activities, there are portions of state government with relatively low levels of expenditures and very little public visibility. The Departments of Agriculture and State Planning, while contrasting sharply in activities, are similar in those two dimensions. Size, however, does not necessarily guarantee anonymity or freedom from controversy. A 1985 proposal by the governor to eliminate the Department of Planning stimulated newspaper editorials, letter writing campaigns, and a debate in the General Assembly.

The list of state departments and their activities underscores the role that the bureaucracy of Maryland plays in the lives of the citizens of the state. We have direct and indirect contacts. We may benefit from certain services and we may question whether others are necessary. An understanding of the overall activities of state government is the necessary basis for making judgments and decisions about the future scope of those activities.

Chapter 7

LOCAL GOVERNMENT IN MARYLAND

The level of government with which citizens are most likely to have direct contact is local government—town, city, county. Yet, the amount of interest and political participation at this level tends to be less than for either the state or national government. In surveys, for example, people are more likely to identify state and national officers than locally elected officials. Similarly, voter turnout in local elections tends to be significantly lower than for other levels.

Nevertheless, the public policy issues that most concern people are those that are dealt with by local governments. Moreover, there are striking and significant examples of political participation at the local level that constitute exceptions to the generalizations about political apathy. Neighborhood and community politics have become an increasingly important part of the American political landscape.[1]

In general, we need to understand two principles about local government in the United States before beginning any overall discussion of the topic. First, local governments are, legally and constitutionally, entirely dependent on the authority of the state. The United States Constitution does not mention local governments anywhere, and it is accepted that they have no legal standing under that document. Local governments are, in the words of one scholar, "mere conveniences of the state."[2] There is a long-standing legal doctrine, known as Dillon's Rule, which states that local governments have only those powers which are expressly granted to them by the state, and that any interpretation of the extent of local powers must assume a narrow and limited authority.[3] In other words, local governments are not sovereign entities. The significance of this dependent condition will be examined more fully with respect to local government in Maryland later in this chapter.

The second generalization about local government in the United States is that the forms are diverse, complex, and often overlapping. We are more inclined to think about what may be called general-purpose government, in which all functions of government are the responsibility of a single, identifiable unit of government. Most often, we think only in terms of the county or city in which we live. At the local level, however, the authority for carrying out public activities is often divided among different governmental units. The most frequent example is the one in which a county government shares responsibilities with a municipal government within its borders. A second common example is the independent school district, which has its own taxing and spending authority, and which is not controlled by other local units. In addition to school districts, there are numerous other kinds of single-function, special-district governments in the United States. As we shall see, the complexity that exists in some areas of the country with respect to units of local government is much less evident in Maryland.

The study of local government in Maryland requires an examination of both differences and similarities among various sections of the state. Statistics about local government revenues and expenditures not only enable numerical comparisons, but also raise important public policy questions. To what extent should differences in either needs or resources on a geographical basis result in significantly different levels or types of local government services? This question may be either a legal or a political one depending on the particular service in question.

To answer this question also focuses attention on the appropriate role of the state in dealing with local issues. State government is involved in local government matters in all sorts of ways, but it also delegates important questions to the sole discretion of local governments. The balance between the state and the local role is subject to continuing debate and discussion, and to change. Specific examples will be discussed in the following sections in an effort to highlight this issue.

The Structure of Maryland Local Government

In the United States, there are 82,341 units of government. One unit is the federal government, fifty are state governments, and the remaining 82,290 (as of 1982) are various forms of local governments. The particular patterns of government structure vary enormously from

Table 7-1. NUMBER OF GOVERNMENTS IN THE UNITED STATES

Type of Government	1972	1977	1982
U. S. government	1	1	1
State governments	50	50	50
Local governments	78,218	79,862	82,290
Community	3,044	3,042	3,041
Municipal	18,517	18,882	19,076
Township	16,991	16,822	16,734
School districts	15,781	15,174	14,851
Special districts	23,885	25,962	28,588
Total	78,269	79,913	82,341

Source: United States Department of Commerce, Bureau of the Census, *Statistical Abstract of the United States*. Washington, D.C., 1985.

state to state and even within different areas of a single state. The range runs from the high of 6,468 in Illinois to a mere 19 in Hawaii. Maryland is one of the least complicated of states in terms of local governments, with a total of 439, ranking forty-second in the nation.[4]

The distribution of types of local governments for the entire United States is shown in Table 7-1. These various kinds of governmental units differ considerably in their authority and activities, extending from the multipurpose governments that operate with a great deal of autonomy, as the result of a wide-ranging delegation of powers from the state, to the very narrow and specialized single-purpose governments, whose existence and activities may be unknown to most citizens.

In Maryland, the principal unit of local government is the county, of which there are 23. The specific powers and functions of these counties differ and are described below. Maryland has 154 incorporated municipalities, which most people think of as cities or towns. In terms of units of government, there are numerous places with many of the characteristics of towns, including a name and post office identity, that are not self-governing, and receive all of their local governmental services from the county.

The major municipality in Maryland is Baltimore. Baltimore has a unique status within the state, not being within or under the jurisdiction of any county, but, rather, having its own governing charter. In essence, the city of Baltimore is treated by the state as the equivalent of a county. Because of its distinctive characteristics as well as its importance within the state, Baltimore will be discussed more fully in the next chapter.

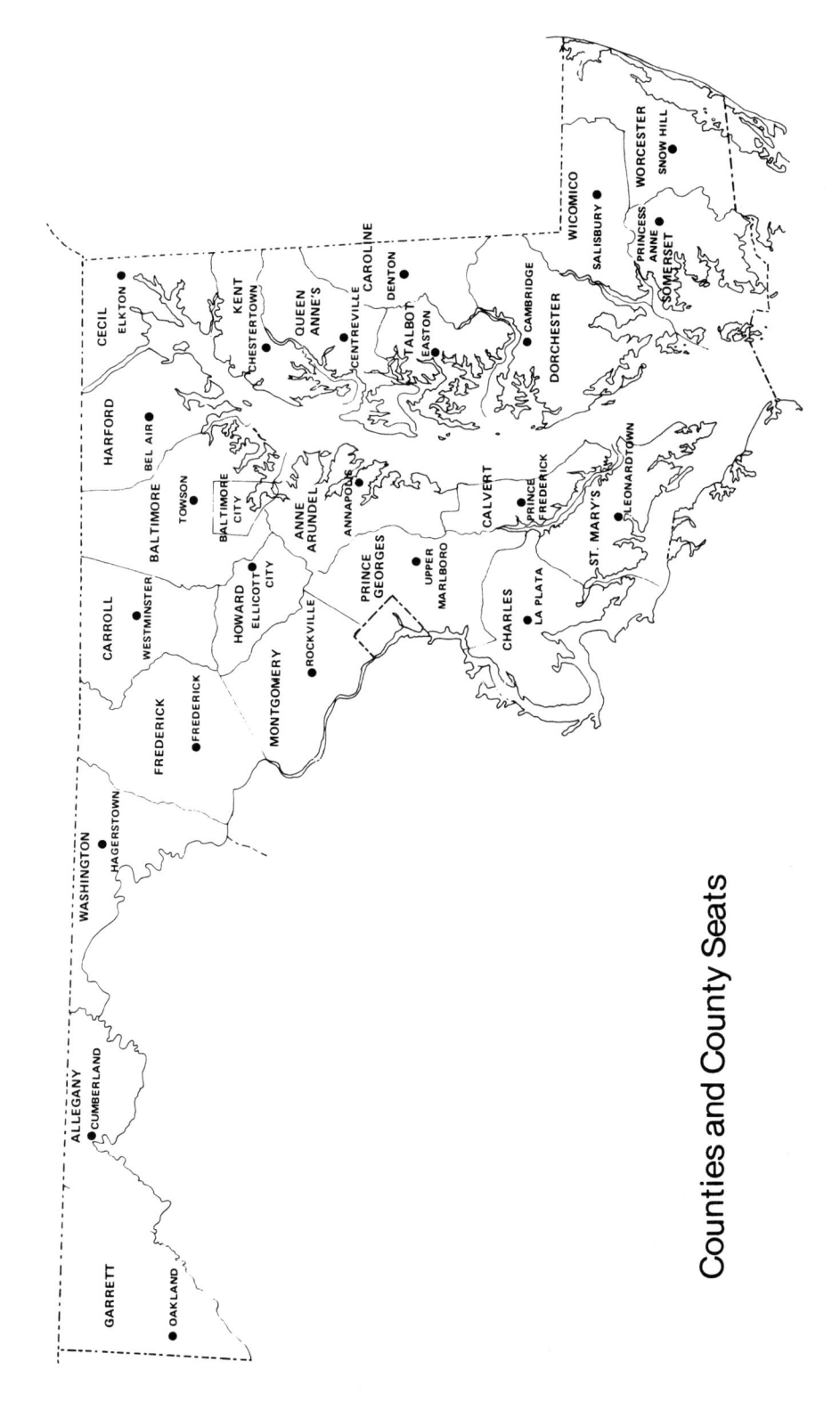

LOCAL GOVERNMENT IN MARYLAND **117**

Counties and County Seats

Of the state's 154 municipalities, only Baltimore with a population of approximately 750,000, is a major city. There are seven municipalities in the state with populations in the range of 25,000 to 50,000. In fact, the second largest incorporated city in Maryland is Rockville, with a population in excess of 43,000. As we will see, county government rather than municipal government is the main type of local government in Maryland, the only exception being that of Baltimore.

As Table 7-1 shows, a frequently used form of single-purpose government in the United States is the school district. In many parts of the country, there are independent school districts, which not only have their own taxing authority but set their own budgets as well. In some instances, voter approval of school bond issues is required, and is often the source of political controversy. Maryland, by contrast, has a system of dependent school districts.[5] The financial needs of the school systems are determined by and provided for through the normal budgetary processes of the county governments or by Baltimore City. In each jurisdiction, there is a local school board which is responsible for the administration of the school system. In eight counties—Allegany, Carroll, Charles, Howard, Kent, Montgomery, Prince George's, and Washington—the school board is locally elected. The Board of School Commissioners in Baltimore is appointed by the mayor, while the remaining school boards are appointed by the governor. Nationally, appointed school boards are very rare. Almost all school districts outside Maryland have elected school boards.

The other principal form of local government in the United States is the special district, a single-purpose unit of government, which is responsible for providing a particular service and which may have an independent taxing authority.[6] The activities of special districts range from the apparently trivial to matters of great local importance. In some parts of the country, water districts, mosquito-abatement districts, or transportation authorities may play important governmental roles. In Maryland, there are 264 special districts, of which 167 are Drainage and Flood Control districts. Again, these numbers reinforce the fact that most governmental services in Maryland at the local level are provided by county government or its equivalent.

One other observation about the pattern of local government in Maryland is worth noting. The relatively small number of units of local government means that the overlapping of authority among governmental entities and the fragmentation of responsibility among them are avoided. Most governmental services in Maryland are provided by

NAMES AND ORIGINS OF MARYLAND COUNTIES

		Derivation of Name	County Seat
Allegany	1789	Oolikhanna, beautiful stream	Cumberland
Anne Arundel	1650	Wife of Cecil, second Lord Baltimore	Annapolis
Baltimore City	1850	(Was part of Baltimore County until 1850, when it became a separate political division of the state)	
Baltimore County	1659	Proprietor's Irish barony	Towson
Calvert originally Patuxent	1654	Family name of the Proprietary	Prince Frederick
Caroline	1773	Sister of the last Lord Baltimore, Lady Caroline Eden	Denton
Carroll	1835	Charles Carroll of Carrollton	Westminster
Cecil	1674	Second Lord Baltimore	Elkton
Charles	1658	Charles Calvert, son of Cecil, second Lord Baltimore	La Plata, but Port Tobacco until 1895
Dorchester	1668/9	Earl of Dorset, friend of the Calverts	Cambridge
Frederick	1748	The last Lord Baltimore	Frederick
Garrett	1872	John W. Garrett	Oakland
Harford	1773	Henry Harford, last Proprietary	Bel Air
Howard	1851	Colonel John Eager Howard	Ellicott City
Kent (probably)	1640	Kent County, England	Chestertown
Montgomery	1776	General Richard Montgomery	Rockville
Prince George's	1695	Prince George of Denmark, husband of Queen Anne of England	Upper Marlboro
Queen Anne's	1706	Queen Anne of England	Centreville
St. Mary's	1637	Mary, the mother of Jesus	Leonardtown
Somerset	1666	Mary Somerset, Sister of Cecil, second Lord Baltimore	Princess Anne
Talbot	1661	Grace Talbot, daughter of George, first Lord Baltimore	Easton
Washington	1776	General George Washington	Hagerstown
Wicomico	1867	Wicko-mekee, village on a stream	Salisbury
Worcester	1742	Earl of Worcester	Snow Hill

Source: *Maryland Manual,* Hall of Records Commission, Annapolis, and Edward B. Matthews, *The Counties of Maryland,* Maryland Geological Survey, Special Publication vol. III, Part 5, Baltimore, 1907.

general-purpose county governments rather than by single-purpose special districts. By contrast, in the San Francisco area, in which there are over five hundred units of local government of one type or the other, both the determination of responsibility for particular services and the coordination of different governmental activities are much more difficult. While simplicity of structure does not insure effective government, most studies conclude that complexity can be a barrier to it.

Powers of Local Government

It is worth repeating that all powers of local governments are delegated from the state. Local governments are not sovereign. These basic legal and constitutional truths need, however, to be considered in the context of some equally basic political and economic truths.

Local control over local issues has always been an important political value in the United States. Resistance to a faraway, central authority goes back to the American Revolution. While conditions have certainly changed dramatically since the eighteenth century, the desire for local control continues to have strong support. To cite one example, local communities have been very resistant to either federal or state intervention in the running of public schools. Similarly, efforts at centralizing land-use planning have met with considerable local opposition. The Eastern Shore's opposition to the proposal of the state's Critical Areas Commission in 1986 to limit future development in areas contiguous to the Chesapeake Bay is a recent example of this sentiment. Attempts to maintain local control have not always been successful, nor have supporters of the principal of local control always been consistent in their views, at times advocating centralized policy-making on selective issues. Nevertheless, the value attached to local control in this country has meant that state and federal officials have often delegated and deferred to local governments.

The example of local control of schools provides another perspective on the same issue. If a local government does not have adequate resources for providing the level and quality of education that is needed, the appearance of local autonomy in school decision-making may not have much real value. Local control is an illusion if there is no ability to make real choices. In this situation, local governments with a high degree of legal autonomy may end up being dependent on external funding sources and not really in control of the decision-making process. With these perspectives in mind, we can turn to an examination of the formal authority of local government in Maryland.

Norman Harrington

Future development on the Eastern Shore will be affected by the rules proposed by the Critical Areas Commission to clean up the Chesapeake Bay. Shown is St. Michaels, Maryland.

The Maryland Constitution is the basis of all local powers and specifies the manner in which local governments can establish their authority.[7] At the present time, there are four forms of local government in Maryland, although there are similarities among them. Baltimore City, which has been an incorporated municipality since 1797, is governed by a home rule charter, the current version of which was adopted in 1964. While the authority for home rule in Baltimore is found in Article XI-A of the Maryland Constitution, which was ratified in 1915, the city had actually been granted broad powers of self-government as early as 1898 by the General Assembly.

Eight counties—Montgomery in 1948, Baltimore in 1956, Anne Arundel in 1964, Wicomico in 1964, Howard in 1968, Prince George's in 1970, Harford in 1972, and Talbot in 1973—have adopted charter forms of government under the same general constitutional authority as that of

Baltimore City. Under Article XI-A, a county may draw up and adopt its own charter, establishing its system of local government within the guidelines contained in that article. The powers available to home rule governments are specified in the Express Powers Act, which was originally passed by the legislature in 1918 subsequent to the adoption of the Home Rule Amendment to the Constitution.

Three additional counties—Kent in 1970, Allegany in 1974, and Worcester in 1976—have adopted what is known as code home rule powers, a more limited form of local authority under the Maryland Constitution. The authorization for code home rule comes from Article XI-F of the Maryland Constitution, which was added in 1966. This form of charter government, which is easier to adopt than home rule, allows the county commissioners to operate under a broad delegation of authority from the General Assembly.

The remaining twelve counties have retained the county commissioner system, in which all local authority is delegated from the state. While these counties are, in a strict sense, merely administrative subdivisions of the state, they do in fact exercise a significant number of governmental powers. Their authority may, however, be taken back by the state at any time.

There is, in addition, a provision in the Maryland Constitution for municipal home rule. This authority is contained in Article XI-E, which was added to the Maryland Constitution in 1954. The purpose of this amendment was to allow cities and towns greater autonomy in dealing with local matters. While there are, at present, 154 cities operating under the provisions of municipal home rule, the state's largest city, Baltimore, does not derive its authority from Article XI-E simply because, as we've noted, it already had been granted charter government in 1898.

The specific scope of local governmental authority results from the particular provisions of the Maryland Constitution and the relevant charters and codes for each jurisdiction. Baltimore City has the authority to exercise the full state police powers as the result of the 1898 legislation. The Express Powers Act, which applies to all the home rule charters adopted under Article XI-A, contains a specific set of powers. These include the power to acquire, hold, and dispose of county property, to establish county institutions, to contract, zone, and plan, and to levy taxes. Code home rule counties have general grants of power from the legislature, as do incorporated municipalities. But in general, state sovereignty and Dillon's Rule apply, that is, where there is no specific grant of authority, there is no governmental power.

The Courthouse in Frederick County

The actions of local governments are at times challenged in the courts as exceeding their legitimate authority. As an illustration, over a number of years Baltimore banned "For Sale" signs on residential properties. This was contested and eventually disallowed.[8] Local governments end up going to the Maryland General Assembly on some issues to request authority to engage in activities that are not specifically delegated to them. An example is the growing involvement of local governments in economic development, which has required authorization from the state.

Another limitation on local authority, discussed in Chapter 3 on the legislature, stems from the circumstance that the General Assembly may pass legislation that has the effect of local law. It may also pass legislation that preempts local action. For example, the General Assembly adopted a measure in 1984 which overrode the authority of local governments to pass gun control bills. An additional limitation on local authority is the requirement that state constitutional amendments be voted on and approved by all the voters of the state, even if they apply only to a single jurisdiction.

Despite the formal limits discussed above, it is nevertheless the case that local government in Maryland performs important functions and exercises a great deal of authority. The actions of local government have a much greater direct impact on most citizens than do those of state government. The things we complain about as well as the services we depend on are usually performed by local government. The involvement of state government in those activities is more likely to relate to either the financing or the broad policy making than to the actual delivery of the service. A closer look at what local government actually does, as well as what role the state government plays in those local activities, is the focus of the next section.

The Organization and Activities of Local Government

The same set of organizational distinctions that were used to describe Maryland state government can be employed in examining local governments as well. The unit of analysis for this discussion is county government, which, we've pointed out, is the principal form of local government in Maryland. While there are differences from county to county, based in part on the variations in legal authority discussed above, it is still possible to identify common characteristics of all counties.

The legislative authority in each county resides in either the county council or in the board of county commissioners. The latter group also exercises executive authority. There are variations in the home rule counties, with six of them, as well as Baltimore City, having an elected chief executive. The local courts, described in Chapter 6 on the judicial branch, are largely independent of local government.

In each jurisdiction, a portion of government is concerned with the maintenance of governmental operations. Budget and personnel offices clearly fall into this category. In addition, the activities of planning and public works agencies also deal with government maintenance.

The specific governmental functions, with corresponding organizations, will differ from county to county, depending on the characteristics and needs of the area. Obvious bases for differences include: whether the county is urban, suburban, or rural; the level of income and wealth; the major components of the economic base; and the socioeconomic characteristics of the population. Local governments have little or no control over many of these factors, yet they must deal with and respond to them.

A meeting of the Baltimore County Council

The most direct way to examine governmental activities of local government in Maryland is to review the budgets of the counties. The expenditures of local government, divided into major categories, are shown in Table 7-2. The range and the disparities are striking. The total expenditures vary from Baltimore City's $1½ billion to Kent County's $13 million. To emphasize these differences further, it is worth noting that Baltimore City spends almost as much for libraries as the total Kent County budget.

The differences in expenditures in Table 7-2 in part reflect the range of population of the counties. They also reflect the characteristics and needs of those jurisdictions as well as the varieties of available resources. There are numerous examples of these points. Nine jurisdictions support public hospitals; the remainder have no expenditures in this category. A number of counties do not spend money on urban development, housing, or economic opportunity. On the other hand, Baltimore City, which has the largest population in the state, does not have the highest expenditure level in all categories, including education, which is the largest category statewide.

Budget figures can, of course, be calculated in a number of different ways. Table 7-3 indicating the percent of the total budget represented by each category, enables a comparison of the relative priorities of the different jurisdictions. This table also allows us to compare elements that are not affected by the differences in size of the counties and their budgets. A third perspective is provided by the last budget table (Table 7-4) which contrasts per capita expenditures for each of the budget categories. The numbers in this table are not related directly to the population of the counties and, thus, allow a comparison of the priorities of local governments. None of these tables offers a complete picture; each adds to our understanding of the budget and policy choices made by local governments.

A budget is a statement of expenditures and revenues. Local governments in Maryland are obligated to have a balanced budget each year. The differences in expenditure levels reflected in the previous tables have a parallel in the differing revenue bases that local governments have available to them. The sources of local funds are determined by the state, which defines the taxing authority of local government. Historically, the principal source of local revenues has been the property tax. As Table 7-5 shows, that continues to be the case in Maryland today. Revenues obtained from the property tax are determined by two factors, the tax rate, which is established by the local government, and the value of the property being taxed, referred to as the assessable base. Wealthy counties, that is, ones with a high assessable tax base, are able to raise large amounts of tax revenues with less tax effort than poorer counties. For example, County A, with an assessable base of $1 million can generate $20,000 with a tax rate of $2 per $100 of assessed value. County B, with an assessable base of $500,000, would have to have twice the tax rate, or $4, to raise the same amount of money. Although the numbers in this example are obviously just illustrative, the differences among counties are very real.

The property tax is the means by which a local government balances its budget. That is, because the property tax rate can be controlled by the local government, it will determine its anticipated expenditures and its revenues from other sources, and then calculate how much is needed from property taxes to balance the budget. However, this process results in problems for some local governments. The amount of assessable base in a jurisdiction is not necessarily related to the demands for governmental services in that area. Thus, some jurisdictions have to tax at a very high rate in order to generate the necessary funds for their budget. At some point, a high tax rate may persuade both home owners

Part of Maryland's heritage, Drum Point Lighthouse, is now a museum in St. Michaels.

and businesses to relocate to another jurisdiction which has a lower tax rate. The county from which those people are moving is then in an even worse situation because its assessable base has been reduced, forcing it to raise its tax rate even more to produce the same amount of revenues.

Local governments do have other sources of revenues, but they constitute a smaller amount than the property tax, and usually do not help overcome the problem of disparities between wealthy and poor counties. The income tax, which is collected by the state, provides about half the revenues of the property tax. Other local taxes and fees, such as entertainment taxes and parking fines, generate revenues for local government, but are relatively small in their total amount.

To the extent that there is a remedy for the problem of a mismatch between local revenues and the needs of local governments, it comes in the form of intergovernmental transfer payments from both the state and the federal government to local governments. There are a wide assort-

Table 7-2. COUNTY EXPENDITURES BY FUNCTION, FISCAL YEAR 1984

	General Government	Public Safety[a]	Public Works[b]	Public Health Welfare[c]
MARYLAND	300,580,060	587,591,507	857,225,934	671,463,944
Allegany	1,861,267	1,249,320	8,244,340	12,462,715
Anne Arundel	25,256,550	44,636,936	50,791,743	29,832,747
Baltimore City	71,743,897	219,633,222	271,905,214	349,343,720
Baltimore	40,525,531	78,651,212	116,194,480	50,104,666
Calvert	2,473,077	3,326,677	3,469,705	4,665,944
Caroline	757,749	952,721	1,571,424	2,921,495
Carroll	7,149,878	5,625,560	9,449,810	7,811,198
Cecil	2,055,818	3,943,024	4,695,458	5,991,107
Charles	2,631,855	7,370,215	6,631,397	8,794,517
Dorchester	973,025	848,465	3,557,472	4,375,496
Frederick	10,605,140	3,424,964	13,221,598	12,581,748
Garrett	900,505	813,403	6,820,273	3,435,525
Harford	6,774,261	8,886,928	14,097,348	18,016,809
Howard	16,217,128	18,487,538	24,076,457	7,019,830
Kent	785,296	617,035	1,363,480	2,442,885
Montgomery	49,982,616	104,362,952	166,110,776	54,979,569
Prince George's	43,530,438	72,985,502	124,329,559	57,219,369
Queen Anne's	1,040,132	1,107,605	3,748,421	3,444,003
St. Mary's	1,948,674	2,252,434	4,812,850	6,763,839
Somerset	683,380	548,758	2,220,848	3,082,568
Talbot	738,745	940,830	1,381,703	2,625,666
Washington	8,582,774	2,922,029	8,687,855	9,767,133
Wicomico	1,813,984	2,321,893	4,523,486	10,256,304
Worcester	1,548,340	1,682,284	5,320,237	3,525,091

Source: Maryland Department of Fiscal Services, *Local Government Finances in Maryland*, March 12, 1985.

[a] Includes police protection, fire protection, and corrections.
[b] Includes highways, sanitation, waste removal, and other public works.
[c] Includes health, hospitals, and social services.
[d] Includes urban development and housing, economic development, and economic opportunity.

ment of grant programs, some for specific purposes and others more general in nature, that have been developed to assist local governments. Examples include federal revenue sharing, which can be used for almost any local purpose: federal categorical grants, such as the Urban Develop-

Education	Community & Economic Development[d]	Debt Service	Other	Total Expenditures
2,325,197,565	201,195,651	449,512,627	337,619,252	5,730,386,940
38,080,234	922,580	3,467,156	1,900,370	68,187,982
196,836,831	4,397,661	42,555,481	16,121,453	410,429,402
344,367,294	142,696,085	96,898,353	47,542,166	1,544,129,961
342,601,674	7,527,160	58,557,803	78,025,474	772,188,000
25,773,339	322,841	1,854,608	3,123,813	45,010,004
11,705,117	312,524	659,145	1,016,861	19,897,036
51,623,942	370,479	2,883,170	6,007,164	90,921,201
38,295,773	629,944	1,895,716	1,782,156	59,238,996
55,093,142	1,048,502	4,971,092	4,476,203	91,016,923
17,333,665	182,610	1,438,434	1,118,766	29,827,933
69,182,769	2,522,140	3,543,936	2,350,377	117,432,672
15,674,224	262,991	913,770	685,706	29,506,407
83,676,866	1,520,286	8,732,120	5,373,485	147,073,103
87,917,241	1,058,354	32,569,582	10,815,397	198,161,527
7,644,630	7,194	316,266	689,636	13,866,722
416,687,473	20,363,395	110,735,055	65,123,851	989,355,687
345,152,091	13,356,327	64,935,838	75,039,616	796,548,740
14,795,611	1,626,597	726,740	1,253,277	27,742,416
33,407,788	347,710	4,763,156	3,312,716	57,609,167
9,161,545	371,946	273,169	491,749	16,833,963
12,325,770	0	456,227	1,430,217	19,899,158
55,771,287	0	2,223,382	3,284,409	91,238,869
31,771,049	140,914	3,310,128	3,172,871	57,310,629
19,313,200	1,207,381	832,300	3,531,209	36,960,042

ment Action Grant program (UDAG), which is intended to stimulate economic redevelopment in urban areas; federal crop subsidy programs; federal and state aid for transportation systems such as highways and mass transit; state aid for public education; and state assistance for local police departments. The list is not intended to be all inclusive, but, rather, to illustrate the kinds of aid that are provided to local governments.

How much aid should be provided, for what purposes, and how it should be distributed are all matters of continuing debate and discussion within the political system. Federal budget deficits have resulted in

Table 7-3. COUNTY EXPENDITURES BY FUNCTION, PERCENT OF TOTAL, FISCAL YEAR 1984

	General Government	Public Safety[a]	Public Works[b]	Public Health Welfare[c]	Community & Economic Development[d]	Education	Debt Service	Other[e]
MARYLAND	5.25	10.25	14.96	11.71	3.51	53.22	7.84	3.13
Allegany	2.73	1.83	12.09	18.27	1.35	55.84	5.08	2.78
Anne Arundel	6.15	10.88	12.38	7.26	1.07	47.96	10.37	3.93
Baltimore City	4.65	14.22	17.61	22.63	9.24	22.31	6.28	3.07
Baltimore	5.25	10.19	15.05	6.49	.98	44.37	7.58	10.10
Calvert	5.49	7.39	7.71	10.36	.72	57.27	4.12	6.94
Caroline	3.81	4.79	7.90	14.69	1.57	58.83	3.31	5.11
Carroll	7.86	6.19	10.39	8.59	.41	56.78	3.17	6.61
Cecil	3.47	6.66	7.93	10.11	1.06	64.65	3.20	2.92
Charles	2.89	8.10	7.29	9.67	1.15	60.53	5.46	4.92
Dorchester	3.26	2.84	11.93	14.67	.61	58.11	4.82	3.76
Frederick	9.03	2.92	11.26	10.71	2.14	58.91	3.02	2.01
Garrett	3.05	2.76	23.11	11.65	.89	53.12	3.10	2.33
Harford	4.61	6.04	9.59	12.25	1.03	56.89	5.94	3.66
Howard	8.18	9.33	12.15	3.55	.54	44.36	16.44	5.46
Kent	5.66	4.45	9.83	17.62	.05	55.13	2.28	4.98
Montgomery	5.05	10.55	16.79	5.56	2.05	42.22	11.19	6.58
Prince George's	5.46	9.16	15.61	7.18	1.68	43.33	8.15	9.42
Queen Anne's	3.75	3.99	13.51	12.42	5.87	53.33	2.62	4.52
St. Mary's	3.38	3.91	8.35	11.75	.60	57.99	8.27	5.75
Somerset	4.06	3.26	13.19	18.31	2.21	54.42	1.62	2.91
Talbot	3.71	4.73	6.94	13.19	0	61.94	2.29	7.20
Washington	9.41	3.20	9.52	10.71	0	61.12	2.44	3.59
Wicomico	3.17	4.05	7.89	17.89	.24	55.44	5.78	5.54
Worcester	4.19	4.55	14.39	9.54	3.27	52.26	2.25	9.55

Source: Maryland Department of Fiscal Services, *Local Government Finances in Maryland*, March 12, 1985.

[a] Includes police protection, fire protection, and corrections.
[b] Includes highways, sanitation, waste removal, and other public works.
[c] Includes health, hospitals, and social services.
[d] Includes urban development and housing, economic development, and economic opportunity.
[e] Includes recreation and parks, libraries, natural resources, intergovernment, and miscellaneous.

cutbacks in a number of programs that had provided assistance to local governments. Local governments must in turn either find alternative revenue sources or cut back on the programs and services. The activity on the budget at the federal level has resulted in greater attention by local governments to the role that the state might play in helping to overcome the shortfall created by federal reductions. The reality, however, is that local governments have been forced to look much more closely at the services they have been providing, and, as a result, they've had to reduce some programs. The impact of tightening budgets has not affected all jurisdictions to the same extent however. Wealthier counties, with less demand for public services, have been less affected than poorer jurisdictions. This issue is bound to remain a central one in the discussions about the role of government in the coming years.

The Role of Local Government in Maryland

Local government is the level that is closest to the people and is concerned primarily with the direct delivery of services. The great advantage of local government is its proximity to the problems that it is dealing with. Its primary disadvantage is its limited capacity for dealing with those problems. Much of the quandary that local government finds itself in today results from boundaries and geography.

This quandary has two major dimensions. In the first place, local governments compete with each other. In the state legislature, the competition is over the distribution of state funds. There is also competition in attracting businesses to move to a jurisdiction and add to its tax base. On occasion, a regional or even a state perspective may prevail, but competition is the more normal state of affairs.

The second dimension stems from the fact that problems or issues do not stop at political boundaries.[9] The country as a whole has become more aware in recent years of the futility of trying to deal with environmental matters on a local basis. Efforts to clean up the Chesapeake Bay involve not only Maryland, but other states and the federal government as well. In the realm of economic development, businesses focus on a broader geographical area than the specific location of their plant or corporate headquarters. Yet, the local jurisdiction in which it is located may derive far greater economic benefits than the surrounding counties which are also contributing to the economic success and well-being of the business. Even more controversy is generated by the distribution of social service costs. Does one local government bear all the responsibility

Table 7-4. COUNTY EXPENDITURES BY FUNCTION IN DOLLARS PER CAPITA FISCAL YEAR 1984

	General Government	*Public Safety*[a]	*Public Works*[b]	*Public Health Welfare*[c]
MARYLAND	69.29	135.46	197.62	154.79
Allegany	23.50	15.77	104.10	157.35
Anne Arundel	63.84	112.83	128.39	75.41
Baltimore City	95.90	293.59	368.46	466.97
Baltimore	60.72	117.85	174.10	75.07
Calvert	60.47	81.34	84.83	114.08
Caroline	31.18	39.21	64.67	120.23
Carroll	66.33	52.19	87.66	72.46
Cecil	32.79	62.89	74.89	95.56
Charles	31.26	87.53	78.76	104.45
Dorchester	31.49	27.46	115.13	141.60
Frederick	82.02	26.49	102.26	97.61
Garrett	31.27	28.24	236.82	119.29
Harford	43.96	57.67	91.48	116.91
Howard	115.84	132.05	171.97	50.14
Kent	46.19	36.30	80.20	143.69
Montgomery	82.48	172.22	274.11	90.73
Prince George's	65.17	109.26	186.12	85.66
Queen Anne's	36.12	38.46	130.15	119.59
St. Mary's	31.02	35.87	76.64	107.70
Somerset	35.97	28.88	116.89	162.24
Talbot	27.06	34.46	50.61	96.18
Washington	74.89	25.50	75.81	85.23
Wicomico	26.72	34.20	66.62	151.05
Worcester	46.92	50.98	161.22	106.83

[a] Includes police protection, fire protection, and corrections.
[b] Includes highways, sanitation, waste removal, and other public works.
[c] Includes health, hospitals, and social services.
[d] Includes urban development and housing, economic development, and economic opportunity.
[e] Includes recreation and parks, libraries, natural resources, intergovernment, and miscellaneous.

for providing services to poor and needy individuals because a disproportionate number of them live in that jurisdiction?

State aid and state programs are one means to deal with the anomalies of political boundaries at the local level. Efforts at regional

Education	Community & Economic Development[d]	Debt Service	Other[e]	Total
536.04	46.38	103.63	53.23	1,321.07
480.81	11.65	43.78	23.99	860.96
497.57	11.12	107.57	40.75	1,037.49
460.32	190.75	129.53	63.55	2,064.07
513.34	11.28	87.74	116.90	1,157.01
630.15	7.89	45.34	76.37	1,100.49
481.69	12.86	27.13	41.85	818.81
478.89	3.44	26.75	55.74	843.42
610.78	10.05	30.23	27.62	944.80
654.31	12.45	59.04	53.16	1,080.96
560.96	5.91	46.55	36.20	965.31
535.05	19.50	27.41	18.16	908.22
544.24	9.12	31.73	23.81	1,024.53
542.97	9.86	56.67	34.87	954.40
627.98	7.57	232.64	77.25	1,415.44
449.68	.42	18.60	40.58	815.69
689.27	33.60	182.73	107.47	1,632.60
516.70	20.00	97.21	82.34	1,192.44
513.74	56.48	25.23	43.52	963.28
531.97	5.54	75.85	52.75	917.34
482.19	19.58	14.38	25.89	886.00
451.49	0	16.71	52.39	728.91
486.66	0	19.40	28.66	796.15
467.91	2.07	48.75	46.74	844.04
585.25	36.59	25.22	107.02	1,120.00

cooperation are another. Some states have ended up creating metropolitan or regional governments as well as special districts that encompass several political jurisdictions.[10] This approach has not yet had an impact in Maryland. There have been examples of limited cooperation, however, in such areas as fire protection and police coordination among adjacent jurisdictions.

The idea of local control has been associated with specific and permanent political boundaries. Unfortunately, neither resources nor needs neatly conform to those boundaries. In Maryland, as in the rest of

Table 7-5. COUNTY REVENUES BY SOURCE IN DOLLARS, FISCAL 1984

	Property Taxes	Income Taxes	Other Local Taxes	State Shared
Maryland	1,397,922,429	732,802,646	375,742,079	215,049,700
Allegany	13,954,843	7,659,961	830,794	2,534,803
Anne Arundel	109,466,111	69,521,431	30,453,458	11,253,912
Baltimore City	271,513,652	84,251,492	54,977,659	103,599,585
Baltimore	213,278,752	131,969,361	54,182,993	20,642,816
Calvert	22,779,181	2,374,567	480,070	1,458,471
Caroline	3,527,470	2,523,556	117,680	1,514,384
Carroll	22,069,795	16,569,464	2,702,422	3,967,511
Cecil	14,252,473	7,637,758	716,816	2,654,678
Charles	21,779,884	12,679,520	2,959,902	2,872,202
Dorchester	6,172,090	2,934,442	221,201	1,683,541
Frederick	29,024,668	18,903,269	2,514,727	4,630,618
Garrett	6,792,830	2,228,785	742,622	1,979,280
Harford	37,122,177	23,560,740	3,460,461	4,598,386
Howard	53,928,882	32,237,854	17,718,527	4,366,511
Kent	3,830,352	2,126,735	330,848	860,099
Montgomery	287,235,249	164,554,690	149,190,233	15,822,429
Prince George's	210,099,934	112,217,196	45,344,492	16,083,096
Queen Anne's	6,843,810	3,654,320	480,796	1,638,224
St. Mary's	11,015,014	7,684,236	1,338,021	2,625,162
Somerset	2,809,760	1,428,353	278,353	1,097,163
Talbot	5,609,417	3,057,475	382,492	1,278,134
Washington	19,813,611	13,402,418	1,010,606	3,534,479
Wicomico	12,015,655	8,145,050	649,909	2,604,908
Worcester	12,987,299	1,479,973	4,647,069	1,794,313

[a] Federal aid includes federal revenue sharing.
[b] Includes state aid.
[c] Includes fines, forfeitures, misc. revenues, service charges, and debt proceeds.

the United States, there is a need to overcome the geographical barriers associated with local government while at the same time preserving the benefits of local decision-making. Blending those two objectives has not always been easy and has required a constant process of adjustment. Many of the key issues of Maryland politics are centered on that process of adjustment regarding the responsiveness and capabilities of local government.

Licenses and Permits	Federal Aid[a]	Inter-government Aid[b]	Other[c]	Total
39,559,067	654,311,415	1,360,856,038	1,159,696,858	5,935,940,232
222,768	9,719,989	22,388,089	14,832,829	72,144,176
5,136,129	34,443,825	103,086,210	89,771,340	453,168,416
9,632,479	321,852,859	421,711,010	285,168,072	1,552,703,808
4,272,147	55,843,365	143,613,923	170,924,459	794,726,816
97,350	3,873,896	9,989,529	4,151,291	45,204,365
104,360	2,752,246	8,374,201	926,261	19,840,158
458,301	7,332,844	31,000,940	7,645,948	91,747,225
336,637	5,766,881	24,211,798	5,319,968	60,897,009
309,205	7,951,520	30,146,159	12,540,268	91,193,610
36,795	3,979,787	12,185,396	2,329,167	29,542,419
515,429	9,568,730	38,176,699	16,037,648	119,371,788
91,763	4,055,900	11,795,523	1,649,649	29,336,352
688,167	14,698,729	46,272,735	18,058,261	148,459,656
1,910,297	7,816,686	32,220,042	67,392,113	217,590,912
111,918	1,897,295	5,032,235	781,125	14,970,607
6,272,146	61,829,361	109,257,999	227,478,891	1,021,640,998
7,683,506	66,291,993	206,025,450	537,510,652	854,883,579
166,473	2,733,634	10,242,245	21,658,286	30,017,788
264,276	5,191,070	20,475,776	7,675,389	56,268,949
39,174	3,597,675	6,876,490	988,789	17,117,685
152,075	2,146,710	5,612,073	1,812,831	20,051,207
313,482	11,135,094	33,238,481	6,226,823	88,674,994
195,240	6,764,916	19,473,846	18,365,181	68,224,700
546,950	3,072,410	9,447,184	4,187,817	38,163,015

Table 7-6. COUNTY REVENUE BY SOURCE, PERCENT OF TOTAL, FISCAL 1984

	Property Taxes	Income Taxes	Other Local Taxes	State Shared Taxes	Licenses and Permits	Federal Aid[a]	Inter Government Aid[b]	Other[c]
MARYLAND	23.55	12.35	6.33	3.62	0.67	11.02	22.92	19.54
Allegany	19.34	10.62	1.15	3.51	0.31	13.48	31.03	20.56
Anne Arundel	24.16	15.34	6.72	2.48	1.13	7.60	22.75	19.82
Baltimore City	17.49	5.43	3.54	6.67	0.62	20.72	27.16	18.36
Baltimore	26.84	16.61	6.82	2.60	0.54	7.02	20.07	21.51
Calvert	50.39	5.25	1.06	3.23	0.22	8.57	22.10	9.18
Caroline	17.78	12.72	0.59	7.63	0.53	13.87	42.21	4.67
Carroll	24.06	18.06	2.95	4.32	0.50	8.00	33.79	8.34
Cecil	23.40	12.54	1.18	4.36	0.55	9.47	39.76	8.74
Charles	23.88	13.90	3.25	3.10	0.34	8.72	33.06	13.75
Dorchester	20.89	9.93	0.75	5.70	0.12	13.47	41.25	7.89
Frederick	24.31	15.84	2.11	3.88	0.43	8.02	31.98	13.44
Garrett	23.15	7.60	2.53	6.75	0.31	13.83	40.21	5.62
Harford	25.00	15.87	2.33	3.10	0.46	9.90	31.17	12.16
Howard	24.78	14.82	8.14	2.01	0.88	3.59	14.81	30.97
Kent	25.59	14.21	2.21	5.75	0.75	12.68	33.61	5.21
Montgomery	28.12	16.11	14.60	1.55	0.61	6.05	10.70	22.27
Prince George's	24.58	13.13	5.30	1.88	0.90	7.75	24.10	22.35
Queen Anne's	22.80	12.17	1.60	5.46	0.55	9.11	34.12	14.18
St. Mary's	19.58	13.66	2.38	4.67	0.47	9.23	36.39	13.64
Somerset	16.41	8.34	1.63	6.41	0.23	21.02	40.18	5.78
Talbot	27.98	15.25	1.91	6.37	0.76	10.70	27.99	9.05
Washington	22.34	15.11	1.14	3.99	0.35	12.56	37.48	7.02
Wicomico	17.61	11.94	0.97	3.82	0.29	9.91	28.54	26.93
Worcester	34.03	3.88	12.18	4.70	1.43	8.05	24.75	10.97

Source: Maryland Department of Fiscal Services. *Local Government Finances in Maryland*, March 12, 1985.

[a] Includes federal revenue sharing.
[b] Includes states aid.
[c] Includes fines, forfeitures, misc. revenues, service charges, and debt proceeds.

Chapter 8

BALTIMORE CITY

Baltimore is not just another unit of local government in Maryland. It constitutes a distinct category. The city of Baltimore is the only large municipality in the state, with a population of approximately 750,000. All other municipalities rank as small, with Rockville's 43,000 making it a distant second in total population. Moreover, throughout the history of Maryland, Baltimore has occupied a special status. The political and economic development of the state has centered on Baltimore from the colonial period. As recently as the 1940s, the city had almost half the population of the entire state and has been able, as a result, to play an important role in the decision-making of the state government. Similarly, the industrial base of Baltimore has provided the focal point for the state's economy for much of Maryland's history.

Today, there are a number of characteristics of Baltimore that perpetuate its unique position in the state. The needs and problems of the city, many of which are associated with its urban character, are not common to the rest of the state. The programs and policies which the city has developed to respond to those problems also stand out. Indeed, Baltimore has received national attention for its revitalization efforts.

An author of a recent book referred to Baltimore as the "spiritual capital" of Maryland.[1] In reality, however, it is clear that portions of the state do not see themselves as closely tied to Baltimore and do not view either the strengths or the problems of Baltimore as very important to them. This fact is of significance in understanding Baltimore's position within Maryland and its relationship to both state government and other local governments.

In the remainder of this chapter, we will discuss a number of the issues raised in this introduction. We will examine the characteristics of the city and the needs that result from them, the organization and powers of the city government, the recent revitalization that has occurred, and the relationship between Baltimore and other units of government in Maryland. To put the study of Baltimore into perspective, we will begin with a brief discussion of general issues involved in urban government in the United States today.

Are Cities Governable?

In various ways, the problems of large cities have been widely discussed in recent years.[2] For a time, people used the term "urban crisis" to suggest the magnitude of, and lack of ready solutions to, the problems facing large American cities. That expression has fallen out of general use, but the problems it alluded to have remained. Analyses of cities have tended to focus on either the specific substantive problems encountered or on the obstacles to effective governance.

The list of problems specifically associated with large cities is a substantial one.[3] One set of issues relates to poverty. While poverty is not limited to urban areas, the concentrations of poor people in large cities have a substantial impact on the characteristics of cities. Moreover, the needs of poor people place a heavy demand on the resources of urban governments. A number of fundamental policy questions arise as a result. What is government's obligation with respect to the poor? To what extent should that obligation fall solely on the governmental unit in which concentrations of the poor reside? Should policies be developed in which there are means of sharing the responsibility for providing for the needs of the poor? These questions, often controversial, do not even get to the issue of which programs are effective in dealing with the causes of poverty.

A second set of urban issues involves problems that increase in magnitude as the population increases, and which may or may not relate directly to the existence of poverty. Governmental services such as public education, law enforcement, fire protection, and health care change in character when they increase in scale. The existence of poverty magnifies the needs in each of these areas, but the effort to provide these public services is invariably more difficult in large cities than in rural or less populated communities. The key policy question in this set of issues is what is an adequate level and quality of service.

In urban areas the interplay of social classes and racial and ethnic groups is particularly evident. Indeed, there are those who contend that this is the most critical issue in our large cities today, and in society as a whole.[4] The values of fairness and equality which are basic to our constitutional system are seriously threatened by class and racial strife and by discrimination. The tension caused by this strife and discrimination has often been most evident in large cities, although it is less clear that it is caused by urban conditions per se. In a number of cities, politics and elections have in recent years taken on overt racial overtones, which has increased tensions. A key question for cities is whether different groups are able to participate in the political process without polarizing it.

A fourth set of issues facing many large cities can be categorized under the rather imposing label of infrastructure problems. The physical condition of a city and its primary structures can pose serious problems, both in terms of performing certain basic functions and in the cost of improvements which may become necessary. The deterioration of roads and bridges is probably the best-known example, but the need to maintain storm water, sanitary sewerage, utility systems, and others may place substantial burdens on city governments. For the most part, infrastructure problems are associated with older cities, although newer, developing communities are faced with the task of constructing initial infrastructure systems.

These four sets of issues indicate the range and type of problems facing large cities in the United States today. The problems are, in and of themselves, real and substantial. In addition, urban governments have to contend with the cumulative weight and impact of these problems. Whether or not it is possible to devise effective and acceptable solutions to these problems, individually and in combination, lies at the heart of the notion of an urban crisis.[5]

A second approach to the same concern involves an examination of the structure and capabilities of local government. Some analysts, such as Douglas Yates, question whether the organization and powers of urban governments are well suited to dealing with the problems that they are forced to confront.[6] This perspective focuses not on the insolubility of urban problems, but on the mechanisms for attempting to deal with them.

The structure of urban government, and particularly the degree of centralization or decentralization, is one factor to be considered. Fragmentation of authority within city government is a frequently cited defect. The limited extent of local authority is a second. As the previous chapter indicated, local governments are severely constrained by both the state constitutions and court interpretations as to their powers. The disjointed nature of local politics is another barrier to effective local government.

The inadequacy of resources available to urban governments also limits solutions to problems. This deficiency is more complicated than it might at first appear to be. The authority of local governments to generate revenues is legally constrained, as discussed in Chapter 7. The resource base is also limited, and may in fact be diminished by efforts to increase the tax rate.

Moreover, the demand for services, and hence expenditures, is greater on urban governments. The reason for this is twofold. First, the proportion of the population needing governmental services is higher in urban areas than in other locations. This fact also affects the revenue side, because the poor and needy are much less able to contribute to the revenue base of the city. Secondly, a large city is obligated to provide a wide range of services. Cities are less able to control priorities and select one service instead of another. An example may help explain this point, referred to as "municipal overburden."[7] Table 7-2 in Chapter 7 shows that Baltimore spends a smaller proportion of its budget for public education than any of the counties in the state. This fact does not mean that Baltimore officials have decided that schools are less important than have their counterparts in other jurisdictions. Rather, it reflects the reality that the city has a need to spend and provide a number of other services at high levels, some of which other counties are able to reduce or not provide at all.

The problems faced by cities are not all the same. The age of a city may be an important factor, as discussed with reference to infrastructure. The location, in terms of weather, will affect both the services the city needs to provide and the desirability of the area for businesses and residents. Location is also important with respect to access to raw materials, to trade markets, and to labor supply. Size of cities, and whether they are expanding or contracting, is another element influencing their condition. The mix of the population, and the degree and kind of heterogeneity, affect the kinds of problems that will occur.

Are cities governable? It is clear that some cities in the United States are encountering far more serious problems than others. Older urban centers, such as New York City and Cleveland, have confronted severe fiscal difficulties that threatened their solvency. Sunbelt cities seemed to be prospering with no real financial pressures for a number of years, but, more recently, have faced a slowdown in growth and a tightening up of economic prospects. A number of cities have shown evidence of racial and class strife while others appear to be relatively harmonious.

We could go on with a list of comparisons, but a few basic points stand out. First, conditions over which cities have little or no control have a major influence on their viability. Second, conditions change. Many of the cities that are struggling today were prosperous in the past. Similarly, some of the problems associated with older cities are starting to be experienced in the newer, less developed areas. Third, the decisions and choices of public officials and local communities make some difference. Some older cities have adjusted and adapted better than others.

Baltimore, while continuing to have many of the problems associated with any large urban area, is an example of the latter category. *The Washington Post* observed that Baltimore is "the nation's leading symbol of hope for aging industrial cities."[8] In the following sections, we will examine Baltimore, its government, and its relationship to the rest of the state.

A Profile of Baltimore

The characteristics of Baltimore are very similar to those of many of the older urban areas of the northeast.[9] Baltimore developed as a major industrial and transportation center in the latter part of the nineteenth century and the early portion of this century. Port activities have always been of central importance to the economy, as were the railroad connections between the city and other areas. Large industrial plants, the most prominent one being Bethlehem Steel Corporation, were for many years the heart of the local economy and the primary employers in the area.

The population was over half a million at the turn of the century and grew to nearly a million by the post-World War II period. At that point, the city had close to three-quarters of the area's population and over forty percent of the entire state's. The second largest jurisdiction in 1950 was Baltimore County, which had a population of a little more than one-quarter of a million.

Much has changed in the years since 1950, both in terms of total numbers and in the composition of the numbers. The postwar period in the United States saw a general movement from center cities to suburbs, stimulated by a number of factors, including the Federal Housing Administration's and the Veterans Administration's housing assistance for families seeking new homes, and the development of improved highway systems which facilitated commuting. In addition, there was a substantial migration of blacks from rural southern areas to northern cities. A third major pattern since the 1950s was that of significant relocation of a number of industries from the northeast to the sunbelt region. All of these trends took place over a number of years and all have had an impact on the major characteristics of Baltimore.

In terms of population, the city's total increased slightly in the decade of the 1950s as the region's increased substantially. There was a small decline in Baltimore's population in the 1960s and then a larger decline in the 1970s—over thirteen percent—which appears to be continuing, albeit at a slower pace. By the 1980 Census, the city's population was down to about thirty-six percent of the region's and closer to one-fifth of the state total.

The composition of the city's population has also changed significantly. In terms of race, Baltimore is approximately fifty-five percent black and forty-five percent white (as of the 1980 Census). By contrast, the proportions in 1950 were twenty-four percent and seventy-six percent respectively. Moreover, the racial division in the rest of the Baltimore region is strikingly different; with, for example, Baltimore County having only ten percent blacks and Anne Arundel County thirteen percent.

In addition, the growing involvement of blacks in politics and city government is of great significance for the future of Baltimore. As of 1986, it was the largest city in the United States having a black majority that did not have a black mayor. Whether race becomes a political issue in and of itself or whether it is an incidental factor will be of importance in the future evolution of the city.

A second characteristic of the population of Baltimore is the relatively high proportion of poor and needy persons. The city has approximately one-fifth of its residents living below the poverty level. This concentration of poor people has a major impact on city government. As discussed above, there is both a very heavy demand for public services and an absence of a taxable base for the city to tap in order to obtain revenues. One result is that Baltimore is heavily dependent on outside assistance in the form of aid from the federal and the state governments.

With respect to Maryland government, a number of policy questions arise. Aid to Baltimore is, ultimately, derived from tax revenues obtained from residents and businesses in other portions of the state. Whether or not taxpayers in Montgomery County are willing to support programs to aid the poor in Baltimore City is a politically controversial issue. The other side of this question may be: should the poor and needy be more geographically dispersed than they presently are? Again there is controversy. One approach which has been sometimes suggested is that future public housing not be constructed in Baltimore but in other jurisdictions. This idea has not generally been well received, both because of a lack of receptivity in the other subdivisions and because it is argued that there is a need for more public housing within Baltimore for poor residents already living there.

Poverty and need may be the result of a number of different factors. Long term dependency, often due to the absence of education and job skills, has most often been dealt with by various kinds of assistance programs. Unemployment is another cause of dependency and poverty, which may be either short term and temporary, or the result of more permanent changes in the economy such as the closing down or moving of an industry. Programs that attempt to respond to the latter include retraining for new skills and attempts to create new kinds of jobs. Unemployment insurance is the response to the problem of short-term loss of a job. Dependency may also be caused by an inability to work and generate income that is entirely outside the control of the individual. Examples of these kinds of dependents include the aging and the handicapped.

In all of these instances, the number and concentration of poor and needy people are greater in Baltimore than in any other jurisdiction in Maryland. The resultant demand on the city to provide needed services is an enormous strain on the financial resources that are available within the geographical boundaries of Baltimore. Federal and state assistance has helped, but the pressures have remained high. For example, the rate at which Baltimore taxes property is roughly twice that of the second highest jurisdiction in the state.

The public policy question is to what extent are the needs of the poor within Baltimore City the responsibility of the city and to what extent does the rest of the state have an obligation to assist. The answer to the question has remained open for discussion and debate within Maryland's political system.

The third major pattern in postwar America discussed above is the moving of business and industry. Baltimore, an old industrial city, has been forced to adjust to the loss of a number of industries, with the resultant loss of both tax base and jobs. To illustrate, there were over 113,000 manufacturing jobs in Baltimore in 1950; the figure by the mid-1980s was less than half of that. Some firms have moved to the surrounding counties while others have moved out of the region altogether. There has, in fact, been significant growth in the rest of the area.

Meanwhile, in Baltimore, the total number of jobs has declined since 1960 and the composition of available employment has shifted in the direction of service industries. Moreover, the city government has, in recent years, become very active in the field of economic development, setting up a number of agencies whose role is to work with businesses, to assist them in remaining in the city, and to try to attract new companies to Baltimore. One of the most dramatic examples since the early 1970s has been the ability of the city to create a tourist industry. This new industry employs over 16,000 people and generates over $10 million per year in tax revenues. It shows how government assistance and intervention helped alter the economic structure of the area. Today, private investment is moving into the Baltimore tourism market, without government incentives, and is adding to the city's economic base.

THE GOVERNMENT OF BALTIMORE

As we found in Chapter 7, Baltimore has a home rule charter, the current version of which was adopted in 1964. The state, for almost all purposes, treats Baltimore as the equivalent of a county. But, the special character of Baltimore is evident in the Maryland Constitution which includes a number of provisions which refer specifically and exclusively to the City.

The current system of government is the mayor-city council type. The legislative authority of the city is vested in a nineteen-member council. There are six councilmanic districts, each of which elects three members who serve for four-year terms. In addition, the president of the city council is elected at-large from the entire city.

The general powers of the city council are outlined in Article II of the Baltimore City Charter. The council's authority is limited in a number of basic ways. In the first place, the Baltimore City Council, like the Maryland General Assembly, may only reduce the budget which is submitted to it. Secondly, the charter establishes the Board of Estimates rather than the City Council as the principal fiscal body for the city. It is the Board of Estimates that actually prepares the budget which is submitted to the City Council. The Board also approves all contracts and fixes salaries of city employees. Thirdly, the charter allows the mayor to veto ordinances which have been passed by the city council and requires a three-fourths vote of the council to override a veto.

Baltimore's City Hall

In addition, members of the city council have generally treated their positions as part-time. Staff assistance to the council is quite limited. As a result, the city council has, for the most part, deferred to the leadership of the mayor on important issues. The principal role of most members of the council has been to act as a kind of ombudsman for the complaints of their constituents with regard to city governmental services.

Analysts of urban government would refer to Baltimore as having a "strong mayor" system.[10] The formal authority of the mayor under the charter is significant. The veto power relative to the city council was referred to above. The mayor is a member of the Board of Estimates and appoints two of the other members as well, the City Solicitor and the Director of the Department of Public Works. The remaining two members of the board, the President of the City Council and the City Comptroller, are both chosen in citywide elections. In addition, the mayor has the power to appoint municipal officers, which includes department heads and members of boards and commissions. While this latter power is subject to city council approval, the mayor's selections are rarely rejected.

According to the city charter, the mayor "shall be the chief executive office of the City and have general supervision over all municipal officers and agencies." Observers of urban government have commented on the problems that mayors have in actually being in charge of a city bureaucracy, citing such problems as limited formal authority as well as the lack of time to keep up with the activities of thousands of city employees. Moreover, some agencies are expressly granted a degree of independence under the city charter. For example, the city school superintendent is not selected by the mayor, but by the Board of School Commissioners. Members of boards and commissions serve for fixed terms, and may not be removed by the mayor. In addition, as Douglas Yates suggested about cities in general, the ability of a mayor to govern is influenced by scarce resources and the need to confront problems that may not have apparent solutions.

Some mayors are more successful than others in overcoming these obstacles. In Baltimore, an understanding of the city government would not be complete without reference to William Donald Schaefer, who was elected to four consecutive four-year terms of office starting in 1971. Schaefer, with the same formal authority as his predecessors, was able to exercise enormous power within city government and to help bring about dramatic changes in Baltimore during his tenure in office.[11] His achievements demonstrate several important facts about government. First, individual skill and determination can make a significant difference. Second, innovative and creative approaches can sometimes overcome obstacles that seem permanent and insurmountable. (As we will see shortly, Schaefer initiated new approaches to a number of problems facing the city.) Third, longevity in office may enable accomplishments that cannot be achieved in a short term of office.

The structure of Baltimore city government is spelled out in part in the city charter, which indicates a number of specific agencies and their responsibilities. In addition, new departments have been created by ordinance as needs and conditions have changed. The chart, Baltimore City Government Organization, below, shows the current list of these

Mayor William Donald Schaefer talking with participants in a summer youth employment program

agencies and departments. It is possible to divide them into three different types, somewhat similar to the distinctions that were made about state agencies. Departments concerned primarily with the operation and maintenance of city government include Finance, Civil Service, and Law. The other agencies tend to focus their activities primarily on either physical development—such as Public Works and Transit and Traffic—or on human resources and social services—including Education, Social Services, and Urban Services. The line between the two types of departments is not always a sharp and clear one, as is demonstrated by both the Neighborhood Progress Administration, which administers housing, community development, and manpower programs, and the Department of Recreation and Parks, which maintains the city park system and also runs recreation programs.

    The activities of these agencies are important. As we have noted, local government, more than any other level of government, is concerned with the direct delivery of services to citizens.

BALTIMORE CITY GOVERNMENT ORGANIZATION
City Officials—Elected by the Voters

The Executive | The Legislators | Some Members of the Judicial Branch

| Mayor | Comptroller | | President of the City Council
18 City Council Members | | State's Attorney
Circuit Court Judges |

Board of Estimates
Policy-making body of the City
Members are: Mayor, Comptroller, President-City Council, City Solicitor, Director-Public Works

EXECUTIVE DEPARTMENTS
Department Heads Appointed by the Mayor

| Civil Service | Education | Finance | Fire | Health | Neighborhood Progress Adm. | Jail | Law |

| Legislative Reference | Municipal & Zoning Appeals | Planning | Police | Public Works |

| Recreation & Parks | Social Services | Transit & Traffic | Urban Services |

Source: Department of Legislative Reference, *The City of Baltimore Municipal Handbook.*

BOARDS AND COMMISSIONS
Appointed by the Mayor and Confirmed by the City Council

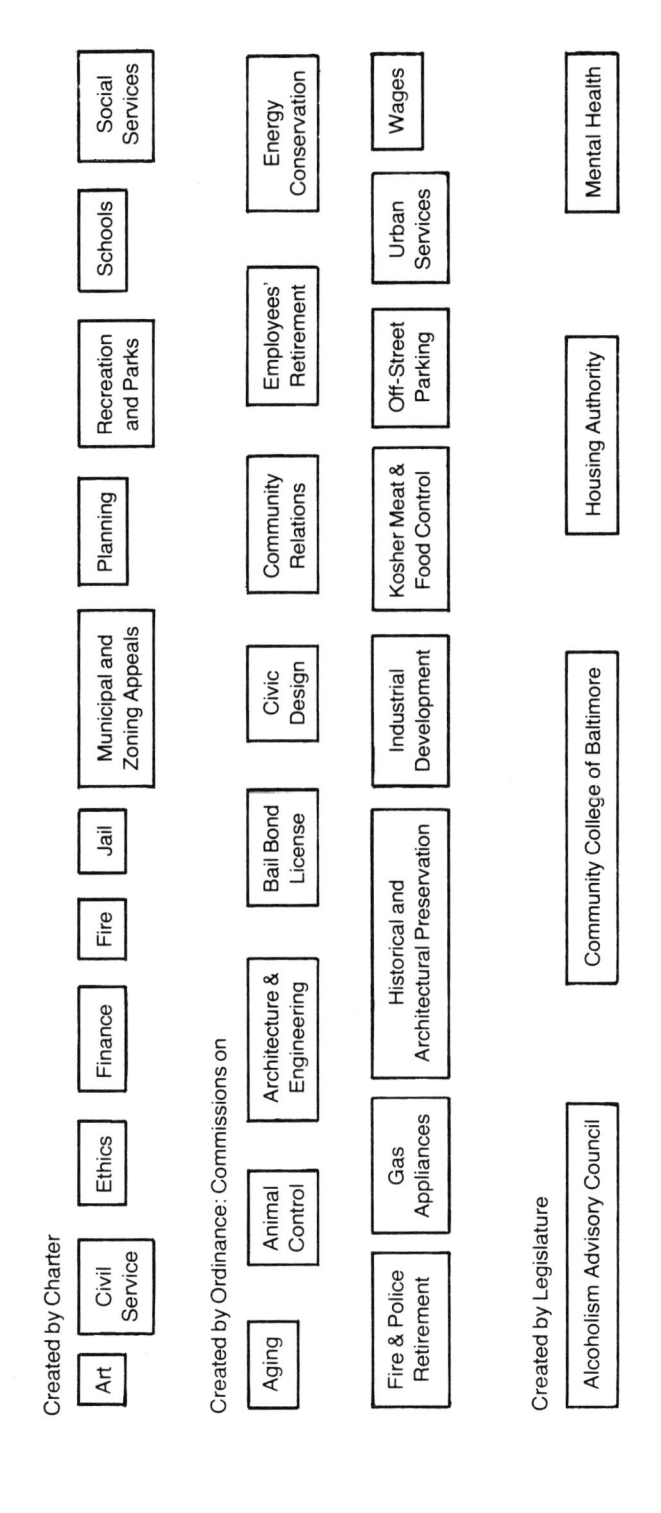

Created by Charter

| Art | Civil Service | Ethics | Finance | Fire | Jail | Municipal and Zoning Appeals | Planning | Recreation and Parks | Schools | Social Services |

Created by Ordinance: Commissions on

| Aging | Animal Control | Architecture & Engineering | Bail Bond License | Civic Design | Community Relations | Employees' Retirement | Energy Conservation |

| Fire & Police Retirement | Gas Appliances | Historical and Architectural Preservation | Industrial Development | Kosher Meat & Food Control | Off-Street Parking | Urban Services | Wages |

Created by Legislature

| Alcoholism Advisory Council | Community College of Baltimore | Housing Authority | Mental Health |

For a fuller understanding of Baltimore and its problems, we need to go beyond the formal structure of its city government. There is a fourth type of activity that has grown in importance but is not adequately dealt with by any of the existing agencies. That area is economic development. The decline in the economic base of the city, the loss of tax revenues and jobs that has accompanied it, and the continuing and growing demand for city services have led a number of cities, including Baltimore, to become directly involved in trying to influence and shape the local economy rather than merely to respond to it.

In Baltimore, new organizations, outside the formal structure of city government, yet tied to it, have been established. The first was the Charles Center-Inner Harbor Management Corporation, which has overseen the redevelopment of downtown Baltimore and the harbor area. A second was the Trustees for the Loan and Guarantee Program, which was a mechanism for financing and supporting development projects. The Baltimore Economic Development Corporation (BEDCO), a third agency, was created to work with private corporations interested in staying in or moving to Baltimore. The fourth is the Baltimore Office of Promotion and Tourism, which has stimulated a new area of economic activity in the city.

All of these organizations operate as part public, part private. Their funding comes from the city, but their operation is independent of most of the city rules and restrictions. While there has, at times, been some controversy about these agencies, particularly in terms of their lack of public accountability, they have also been seen as enormously successful and as examples of creative responses to new problems that the city was not able to deal with through its normal and standard procedures.[12] Finally, all these agencies have been closely tied to the mayor, so that the ultimate form of public accountability has come through public judgments, at elections, on his performance in office.

BALTIMORE'S RENAISSANCE

Baltimore, which occupied a unique and central position in Maryland for so much of its history, experienced a decline in population, wealth, and importance in the third quarter of the twentieth century. The city's relative standing in the state has, without question, been unalterably diminished. Nevertheless, Baltimore has undergone in recent years a dramatic revitalization that has changed its character, enabled it to respond to some of the problems confronting it, and has given the city a new vigor.

Baltimore's Inner Harbor

The visible dimension of the Baltimore renaissance is evident in the new buildings and economic activity of the downtown area and particularly of the Inner Harbor. The Rouse Company's Harborplace, opened in 1980, attracts more visitors each year than Disney World. The National Aquarium, the Maryland Science Center, and the Six Flags Power Plant are major tourist attractions. The Convention Center, built with state financial assistance, has helped turn Baltimore into an active and busy convention city, and stimulated the construction of nearly a dozen hotels in the downtown area. The rate of new office development in Baltimore has increased steadily for the last several years. All this economic activity has added millions of dollars to the city's tax base and has led to the creation of thousands of new jobs. Moreover, a process that was started with a heavy infusion of public money has led to significant private investment in downtown Baltimore.

Baltimore has received a great deal of national attention for its redevelopment program.[13] Cover stories in national magazines, articles by syndicated columnists, and planning and architectural awards have all occurred with increasing regularity. Some of this recognition has focused on public officials, like Mayor Schaefer, but the overall image of the city has also greatly improved. Moreover, many observers have suggested that residents of Baltimore have developed a more positive attitude about their city as well.

The benefits of the Baltimore renaissance extend beyond the harbor area. The entire region has become more attractive to both businesses and residents. New jobs and business opportunities have been created for the residents of the entire area. The state has also received additional tax revenues as a result.

At the same time, it cannot be said that all problems in Baltimore have been solved. Some critics have spoken of there being "two Baltimores," one for those who shop at Harborplace and the other for the poor and disadvantaged. The list of fundamental urban problems remains, from a high crime rate, to a poverty level of twenty percent of the population, to dissatisfaction with the quality of the public school system. Moreover, the city remains financially strapped, heavily dependent on state and federal assistance, the latter of which is being cut, with a high tax rate, and growth which is still less than that of the surrounding counties.

The remaining problems do not mean that the revitalization of Baltimore has not been important or has not had a major impact. It means that the issues confronting urban governments like Baltimore's are substantial. Some would even say that they are unresolvable, or at least beyond the control of local governments. Baltimore's experience in recent years suggests that progress and improvements are possible and that local government may still be viable and effective. It is also clear, however, that both the achievements and the problems of a city like Baltimore are not isolated but, rather, are related to the region and the state of which the city is a part. In concluding this chapter, we will look at the relationship between Baltimore and other units of government in Maryland.

Baltimore and the State

We've seen that Baltimore has a close relationship to the rest of the state and, indeed, that there is an obvious interdependence of the city with the surrounding jurisdictions as well. When Baltimore was the dominant economic center of Maryland, other areas of the state benefited from the spillover effects. Today, there is sustained economic growth in other jurisdictions that is not dependent on Baltimore. Yet, the city, as a core area for the region, albeit a smaller core than it once was, is still important. The economic revitalization described in the previous section testifies to the continued vitality and importance of the city.

Baltimore's problems do not really come from either the fact that it is a smaller portion of the region and of the state than it once was, or from the fact that other areas have achieved significant economic growth and attractiveness for themselves. Rather, in terms of the viability of Baltimore as a governmental unit, the fundamental issue is that the city has a disproportionate share of citizens in need of services. There are four broad approaches available for dealing with this problem.

The first, largely in place today, is to treat the problems of Baltimore specifically and offer piecemeal aid to help lessen the burden. A second possibility is to decide that government does not have any obligation to assist the poor and needy and therefore to cut dramatically the level of services, and hence the expenditures. While it is doubtful that such a choice would be made through the local political processes, the same effect would in fact be achieved if there were significant reductions in state and federal financial aid. The latter cuts have already taken place to some extent.

The other two measures go in quite a different direction. The state, rather than reducing its role, could greatly increase it. Over the years, certain functions of local government have come under more state control and have, in some instances, been fully financed by the state. An example shows up in the debate over what level of financial support Maryland should make for public education. Greater state involvement provides a mechanism for augmenting the resources of jurisdictions with greater needs than finances, but it also jeopardizes the ability of local communities to govern themselves.

The fourth possibility involves a regional approach to government. The political boundaries in the Baltimore area divide both problems and resources. The development of the idea of a metropolitan government is an effort to make the "political city" and the "economic city" coincide.[14] In terms of governance and problem solving, there is a clear logic to this approach, but there is just as clear a political resistance to it. Moreover, the sharing of burdens does not necessarily have widespread appeal.

Of these choices, a continuation of the first approach seems most likely. Long historical traditions, support for the value and benefits of local control, and the absence of a political consensus within the state on any of the other possibilities are the main reasons. The chief virtue of the American system of federalism, with its multiple levels of government, is that it has allowed both experimentation in government and pragmatism in solving problems. As this chapter has described, Baltimore has changed in a number of fundamental ways in recent years, and the governmental system of the city and the state has been flexible in responding to those changes. The need to continue to find a means of dealing with the major problems that are contained within the borders of Baltimore is the ongoing challenge to the governmental system.[15]

Chapter 9

POLITICS AND ELECTIONS

Theories of democratic government emphasize that ultimate power resides in the citizens of the community. This principle is clearly stated in both the U. S. and the Maryland Constitutions. Yet there is considerable evidence that many citizens either do not wish to be involved in the political process or do not believe that they in fact can influence it.[1] The most measurable and easiest form of political participation, voting, is not taken advantage of by a large number of citizens. Involvement in other forms of political participation is even less than for voting.

The specific level and types of political participation vary by state and community. Factors that influence participation include the history, traditions, and attitudes of citizens toward the political process, which political scientists refer to as the "political culture" of an area, as well as the rules and regulations that deal with political participation.[2]

The characteristics of those who do get actively involved in politics are different from those people who are apolitical.[3] Level of education is the single most important factor, but the availability of resources such as time and money is also significant. It is clear that some people are very actively involved in the political process while others are largely indifferent.

Does participation in politics make a difference? Although there are people who are cynical about the political process, there is considerable evidence that real changes in public policy can result, depending upon which candidates are elected to office. Moreover, the expression of opinions and the exerting of pressure on public officials do at times influence decisions. Finally, there are some mechanisms for direct participation in decision-making by citizens. All of this adds up to the potential for a substantial effect.

These general observations set the stage for an examination of political participation in Maryland. The first area to be examined is the role of political parties.

Political Parties in Maryland

Most observers describe Maryland as a solid Democratic party state. The numerical evidence for this conclusion is quite strong:

—Seventy percent of state voters are registered as Democrats.
—Six of the last seven governors have been Democrats.
—The state has voted for the Democratic presidential candidate in five of the past seven elections.
—Six of the eight current members of the House of Representatives are Democrats.
—Ninety percent of the state legislators are Democrats.

Interestingly, these numbers do not mean that Republicans never succeed in important elections in Maryland. Ronald Reagan won the state's vote in the 1984 presidential election. Charles Mathias had no difficulty winning his Senate elections decisively. Helen Bentley defeated incumbent Clarence Long for a seat in the House of Representatives in 1984.

Moreover, many political analysts argue that the role of political parties is becoming less important.[4] The willingness of voters to split their ticket, that is, to vote for candidates of either party depending on the particular office, and the rise in the number of people registering as independents are both indicators supporting the contention that parties are losing their influence.

Historians recall the days of party machines and bosses, when party leaders controlled nominations and could assure voter turnouts that were decisive in elections. For a number of reasons, including the increased importance of television, changes in campaign finance laws, increased voter sophistication, and the growth of government social services, parties have lost the dominant position they once had.

Yet parties do continue to function and to be, at times, important. State laws regulate their activities to a great degree, but, at the same time, insure that they play a continuing part in the election process. What is gone is the control and direct power.

Today, parties organize elections. In Maryland, as in most states, elections are a two-stage process. Both the Democratic and Republican parties nominate candidates for state offices in a primary election, held in September of nonpresidential election years and in the spring of years when there is a presidential election. Maryland has a *closed* primary system, in which participation is limited to those people who have previously registered as members of the party in whose primary they are voting.

A primary may be hotly contested or may have a candidate win a nomination without opposition. As a general pattern, Democratic primaries in Maryland are more often contested, because the Democratic nominee is most often seen as the likely winner of a General Election. For example, numerous candidates entered the 1986 Democratic primaries for both the Senate and the gubernatorial nominations while state Republican party officials were actively searching for candidates to run for these positions.

Candidates in primaries for statewide office are usually individuals who have won elective office before, but there are exceptions. In the modern campaign, candidates put together their own organization, hire political consultants, pollsters, and media specialists, and spend large amounts of money.[5] With access to money, an individual who has not run for political office previously may become a serious candidate. Thus, Maryland Republicans tried to interest such well-known, but nonpolitical figures as columnist George Will and former baseball player Brooks Robinson in running for statewide office in 1986.

Party label is one of a number of factors that voters consider in making election choices. In primaries, the considerations include the positions taken on issues by the candidates, the personality they project, and their record of previous experience. In the General Election, these elements as well as party label may influence the decisions of voters.

The impact of each of these factors is dependent on the particular campaign and on the level of the election.[6] Party organization is more important in some parts of the state in local elections, particularly where voter turnout and interest are not high. An active and well-organized party organization can determine the outcome of some elections.

RECENT ELECTIONS

A brief review of recent elections in Maryland may aid in understanding the political process in the state. Table 9-1 shows the outcomes of the last two presidential elections in Maryland by political subdivi-

Table 9-1. MARYLAND ELECTION RETURNS FOR PRESIDENT OF THE UNITED STATES

	1980		1984	
	Democratic Party Jimmy Carter	Republican Party Ronald Reagan	Democratic Party Walter Mondale	Republican Party Ronald Reagan
MARYLAND	787,935	879,918	726,161	680,606
Allegany	11,143	19,763	12,167	17,512
Anne Arundel	47,565	94,171	50,780	69,443
Baltimore City	202,277	80,120	191,911	57,902
Baltimore	106,908	171,929	121,280	132,490
Calvert	5,455	8,303	4,745	5,440
Caroline	2,198	4,876	2,833	3,582
Carroll	8,898	27,230	10,393	19,859
Cecil	6,681	13,111	7,937	9,673
Charles	10,264	16,132	8,887	11,807
Dorchester	3,160	6,699	4,908	5,160
Frederick	13,411	29,606	13,629	22,033
Garrett	2,386	7,042	2,708	5,475
Harford	17,133	37,382	20,042	26,713
Howard	25,713	35,641	20,702	24,272
Kent	2,390	3,897	2,986	2,889
Montgomery	146,036	146,924	105,822	125,515
Prince George's	136,063	95,121	98,757	78,977
Queen Anne's	2,938	6,784	3,820	4,749
St. Mary's	6,420	11,201	6,773	8,267
Somerset	2,439	4,508	3,342	3,312
Talbot	3,198	8,028	3,995	6,044
Washington	13,329	27,118	14,118	22,901
Wicomico	8,160	16,124	9,431	11,229
Worcester	3,770	8,208	4,195	5,362

Source: Maryland State Archives, Maryland Manual, *General Election Results: November 4, 1980.*

POLITICS AND ELECTIONS

ABSENTEE BALLOT—State of Maryland
SEE WARNING BELOW

ELECTORS FOR PRES AND VICE PRES OF THE UNITED STATES (VOTE FOR ONE)

- WALTER F. MONDALE, Minneapolis, MN / GERALDINE FERRARO, Forest Hills, NY — DEMOCRAT
- RONALD REAGAN, Goleta, CA / GEORGE BUSH, Houston, TX — REPUBLICAN
- DAVID BERGLAND, Costa Mesa, CA / JAMES A. LEWIS, Old Saybrook, CT — LIBERTARIAN
- GUS HALL, Yonkers, NY / ANGELA DAVIS, Oakland, CA — COMMUNIST
- LARRY HOLMES, New York, NY / GLORIA LA RIVA, San Francisco, CA — WORKERS
- DENNIS L. SERRETTE, Jersey City, NJ / NANCY ROSS, New York, NY — ALLIANCE

WARNING

1. MARK BALLOT BY PLACING X IN PROPER BLANK AFTER EACH CANDIDATE OR QUESTION.
2. DO NOT ERASE OR MAKE IDENTIFYING MARK.
3. If your vote for a candidate or question is marked in such a manner that your intent is not clearly demonstrated, your vote for that office or question shall not be counted.
4. In order to protect the secrecy of your vote, do not put your name, initials, or any identifying mark on your official ballot.
5. If it is determined that a ballot is intentionally marked with an identifying mark the entire ballot will not be counted.

THIS BALLOT MUST BE MARKED ONLY AS ILLUSTRATED BELOW.

JOHN DOE — [X]

Use only the "X" — no other mark — to indicate your choice.

FOR REPRESENTATIVE IN CONGRESS THIRD CONGRESSIONAL DISTRICT (VOTE FOR ONE)

- BARBARA A. MIKULSKI — DEMOCRAT
- ROSS Z. PIERPONT — REPUBLICAN
- LAWRENCE K. FREEMAN, Baltimore — INDEPENDENT

FOR JUDGES OF THE SUPREME BENCH 8TH JUDICIAL CIRCUIT (VOTE FOR FOUR)

- EDWARD J. ANGELETTI, Baltimore
- ARRIE W. DAVIS, Baltimore
- ROBERT I. H. HAMMERMAN, Baltimore
- THOMAS E. NOEL, Baltimore

JUDGE, COURT OF SPECIAL APPEALS AT LARGE

ROSALYN B. BELL — FOR CONTINUANCE IN OFFICE
- YES
- NO

QUESTION NO. 1 — CONSTITUTIONAL AMENDMENT

Prohibits certain persons from entering upon the duties of, or continuing to serve in certain elective offices created by or pursuant to the Maryland Constitution if the person was not a registered voter in the State on the date of the person's election or appointment to that term of, at anytime thereafter and prior to the completion of the term, the person ceases to be a registered voter.

- FOR THE CONSTITUTIONAL AMENDMENT
- AGAINST THE CONSTITUTIONAL AMENDMENT

QUESTION A — COMMUNITY DEVELOPMENT LOAN

To authorize the Mayor and City Council to borrow, not to exceed $12,000,000.00, to be used for or in connection with planning, developing, executing, and making operative the Community Development Program of the Mayor and City Council, and for doing any and all things proper or expedient in connection therewith.

- YES
- NO

QUESTION B — MUSEUM LOAN

To authorize the Mayor and City Council to borrow, not to exceed $4,900,000.00, to be used to acquire property, and to construct, erect, modernize, renovate, improve and equip buildings or structures to be or now being used for or in connection with the operations and activities of the Baltimore Museum of Art, the Walters Art Gallery, the Science Center and the Municipal (Peale) Museum.

- YES
- NO

QUESTION C — INDUSTRIAL AND COMMERCIAL FINANCING LOAN

To authorize the Mayor and City Council to borrow, not to exceed $4,000,000.00, to make, contract to make, guarantee or insure financial loans to any person or other legal entity for the purchase, acquisition, construction, reconstruction, erection, development, redevelopment, rehabilitation, renovation, modernization or improvement of industrial and commercial property in Baltimore City.

- YES
- NO

QUESTION D — RECREATION AND PARKS LOAN

To authorize the Mayor and City Council to borrow, not to exceed $2,000,000.00, to acquire land in Baltimore City and thereon, or on other property owned by the City, establish new parks, playgrounds or recreational facilities, and to design, develop, construct, erect, install, protect, enlarge, modernize and equip public park and recreational property, including, but not limited to, the Zoo located in Druid Hill Park.

- YES
- NO

QUESTION E — ECONOMIC DEVELOPMENT LOAN

To authorize the Mayor and City Council to borrow, not to exceed $9,500,000.00, to be used for or in connection with planning, developing, executing, and making operative the commercial and industrial economic development program and the enterprise development program of the Mayor and City Council, and for doing any and all things proper or expedient in connection therewith.

- YES
- NO

QUESTION F — CIVIC CENTER LOAN

To authorize the Mayor and City Council to borrow, not to exceed $2,500,000.00, to make additions and improvements to, and renovate, rehabilitate, modernize and equip the Civic Center in Baltimore City.

- YES
- NO

QUESTION G — CITY JAIL LOAN

To authorize the Mayor and City Council to borrow, not to exceed $12,000,000.00, to be used to acquire property, and to construct, erect, improve, renovate, modernize and equip buildings or structures to be or now being used for or in connection with the operations and activities of the City jail.

- YES
- NO

QUESTION H — SOLID WASTE LOAN

To authorize the Mayor and City Council to borrow, not to exceed $6,000,000.00, to be used for or in connection with planning, developing, and making operative a comprehensive system for the disposal of solid wastes, including establishing, developing, improving and equipping landfill sites and transfer stations, and the construction or erection of new buildings or structures.

- YES
- NO

QUESTION I — HOUSING DEVELOPMENT LOAN

To authorize the Mayor and City Council to borrow, not to exceed $4,000,000.00, to make, contract to make, guarantee or insure financial loans to any person or other legal entity for the purchase, acquisition, construction, reconstruction, erection, development, rehabilitation, renovation, redevelopment or improvement of residential properties in Baltimore City.

- YES
- NO

QUESTION J — RESIDENTIAL FINANCING LOAN

To authorize the Mayor and City Council to borrow, not to exceed $3,000,000.00, to make, contract to make, guarantee or insure financial loans to any person or other legal entity for the purchase, acquisition, construction, redevelopment or improvement of residential properties in Baltimore City.

- YES
- NO

QUESTION K — STREET & BRIDGE LOAN

To authorize the Mayor and City Council to borrow, not to exceed $1,000,000.00, to be used for or in connection with the demolition, removal, relocation, renovation, alteration, construction, improvement and repair of land, buildings, streets, highways, alleys, bridges, utilities or services and other related structures or improvements located within the boundaries of Baltimore City.

- YES
- NO

QUESTION L — SCHOOL LOAN

To authorize the Mayor and City Council to borrow, not to exceed $6,000,000.00, to acquire property in Baltimore City and thereon, or on other property owned by the City, construct, erect and equip new school buildings, athletic and other auxiliary facilities, and for additions and improvements to, or modernization or reconstruction of, existing school buildings or facilities.

- YES
- NO

QUESTION M

Charter Amendment requiring City Council members to live in their district one year prior to their election.

- FOR THE CHARTER AMENDMENT
- AGAINST THE CHARTER AMENDMENT

QUESTION N

Charter Amendment lowering the residency requirement for the Mayor from ten years to one year.

- FOR THE CHARTER AMENDMENT
- AGAINST THE CHARTER AMENDMENT

QUESTION O

Charter Amendment repealing prohibitions against using public funds to construct a stadium other than Memorial Stadium.

- FOR THE CHARTER AMENDMENT
- AGAINST THE CHARTER AMENDMENT

QUESTION P

Petition Proposing to Amend the Charter of the City of Baltimore (1964 Revision, as amended) by amending Section 5(b) of Article VII, to require that members of the Board of School Commissioners of Baltimore be elected by the voters of Baltimore City rather than appointed by the Mayor.

- FOR THE CHARTER AMENDMENT
- AGAINST THE CHARTER AMENDMENT

QUESTION Q

Petition Proposing to Amend the Charter of the City of Baltimore (1964 Revision, as amended) by adding Section 2-A to Article III, requiring that beginning with the Municipal Elections in 1987, each of the eighteen (18) members of the Baltimore City Council shall be elected from a separate District, as established under a redistricting ordinance.

- FOR THE CHARTER AMENDMENT
- AGAINST THE CHARTER AMENDMENT

Voters not present on Election Day are allowed to cast absentee ballots.

sion. Two points stand out. In the 1980 election, the Democratic candidate, Jimmy Carter, was able to carry Maryland even though he won in only four jurisdictions. The margin of his victory came from his 134,000-vote lead in Baltimore. In 1984, Ronald Reagan became the only Republican, other than Richard Nixon in 1972, to win in Maryland since 1956. Reagan reduced the Democratic margin in Baltimore and increased his own majorities in Republican areas.

A second comparison (Table 9-2) can be seen in the last two Senate elections in Maryland, in 1980 and 1982. In the latter race, Paul Sarbanes won reelection in a "normal" Democratic year with a solid sixty-two percent of the total vote. The impermanence of party allegiance is shown by Charles Mathias's equally decisive reelection as a Republican Senator in 1980.

The last two gubernatorial races (Table 9-3) both resulted in clear Democratic victories by Harry Hughes. The numbers in those elections support the view of Maryland as a Democratic state. The competitive nature of politics within the Democratic Party in Maryland is demonstrated by an examination of the 1978 Democratic primary for governor (Table 9-4). The vote was split between three major candidates, Harry Hughes, a former State Senator, Ted Venetoulis, the Executive of Baltimore County, and Blair Lee, the Acting Governor.

A final set of election figures are from the congressional races in Maryland in 1982 and 1984 (Table 9-5). Incumbents usually win contests for the House of Representatives. Maryland is no exception. Not only did the incumbents win fifteen of the sixteen races, but the results were generally one-sided.

The 1986 elections in Maryland confirmed most of these patterns, but also contained one significant change. Democrats maintained their control of the state, winning all of the major statewide offices, including a U. S. Senate seat previously held by a Republican. The Democratic gubernatorial candidate, Baltimore Mayor William Donald Schaefer, collected eighty-two percent of the votes in the General Election to register the most decisive victory in the country.

The major change was the election of four new members to the U. S. House of Representatives and one new U. S. Senator, a turnover of half of Maryland's congressional delegation. This transformation was made possible by three retirements and the decision of two other incumbents to run for higher office, leaving five vacant seats to be contested.

Table 9-2. MARYLAND GENERAL ELECTION RETURNS FOR UNITED STATES SENATOR

	1980		1982	
	Democratic Party Edward T. Conroy	Republican Party Charles McC. Mathias, Jr.	Democratic Party Paul S. Sarbanes	Republican Party Lawrence J. Hogan
MARYLAND	435,118	850,970	707,356	407,334
Allegany	6,829	18,700	12,056	10,503
Anne Arundel	33,028	76,352	52,875	44,199
Baltimore City	83,175	108,051	160,318	32,881
Baltimore	78,694	151,087	118,305	80,834
Calvert	3,096	5,774	5,768	3,614
Caroline	1,571	3,586	3,046	2,237
Carroll	10,285	16,623	10,752	13,844
Cecil	5,101	9,507	8,275	5,992
Charles	6,551	11,308	9,266	6,878
Dorchester	2,520	5,463	4,540	3,136
Frederick	8,143	26,230	13,115	14,230
Garrett	1,609	5,136	3,801	3,067
Harford	12,562	32,805	20,024	18,175
Howard	11,970	31,740	20,819	14,322
Kent	1,419	3,331	3,153	2,129
Montgomery	60,506	196,817	121,589	68,818
Prince George's	79,532	87,311	94,619	42,172
Queen Anne's	2,161	4,730	3,957	3,296
St. Mary's	4,551	7,602	7,265	4,524
Somerset	1,581	2,986	3,218	2,502
Talbot	1,912	6,439	4,124	4,114
Washington	10,220	22,460	13,126	14,696
Wicomico	5,663	11,675	9,240	7,515
Worcester	2,438	5,257	4,105	3,656

Source: State Administrative Board of Election Laws, *General Election Results: November 4, 1980*; Department of General Services, Maryland Hall of Records Commission, *Maryland Manual 1983-1984*.

Table 9-3. MARYLAND GENERAL ELECTIONS RETURNS FOR GOVERNOR

	1978				1982	
	Hughes Bogley	Beall Allen	Goldstein	Devine	Hughes Curran	Pascal Steers
MARYLAND	718,328	293,635	659,415	246,492	705,910	432,826
Allegany	10,534	14,651	11,984	8,783	13,820	9,489
Anne Arundel	59,242	27,119	58,226	19,650	44,002	57,726
Baltimore City	135,108	33,011	120,862	18,425	149,455	47,398
Baltimore	147,404	48,553	140,635	38,064	105,899	100,527
Calvert	5,097	2,003	5,988	1,134	6,316	2,978
Caroline	4,135	1,135	3,592	1,035	3,660	1,940
Carroll	13,254	8,200	12,820	6,462	11,317	14,981
Cecil	8,290	4,231	8,077	3,446	8,608	6,012
Charles	8,563	3,454	7,980	2,876	11,301	4,924
Dorchester	5,980	1,904	5,297	1,372	4,460	3,913
Frederick	14,368	10,373	14,581	7,451	15,495	13,541
Garrett	2,043	4,714	3,312	2,453	3,862	3,258
Harford	22,128	10,196	22,761	7,658	18,902	19,393
Howard	22,287	21,320	7,264	21,476	21,476	14,436
Kent	3,971	1,298	3,780	1,072	3,416	2,041
Montgomery	115,286	54,986	94,400	65,828	131,440	58,807
Prince George's	88,894	29,465	73,232	31,833	104,157	32,504
Queen Anne's	5,167	1,613	4,921	1,342	4,043	3,479
St. Mary's	7,590	2,389	7,229	1,829	7,980	3,607
Somerset	3,967	2,554	3,631	1,687	3,392	2,495
Talbot	5,333	2,374	4,659	2,283	4,772	3,805
Washington	14,891	13,353	17,336	7,852	14,140	14,638
Wicomico	10,350	4,598	8,549	4,794	9,477	7,520
Worcester	4,446	2,300	4,243	1,899	4,520	3,414

Table 9-4. DEMOCRATIC PRIMARY ELECTION RETURNS FOR GOVERNOR—SEPTEMBER 12, 1978

	Hughes Bogley	Lee Hoyer	Orlinsky Young	Venetoulis Stockett
MARYLAND	213,457	194,236	25,200	140,486
Allegany	1,317	2,490	252	4,250
Anne Arundel	20,091	13,726	1,272	10,943
Baltimore City	49,222	44,427	7,645	29,444
Baltimore	70,712	31,819	5,119	24,724
Calvert	987	2,108	127	1,269
Caroline	1,832	541	66	466
Carroll	4,682	2,017	359	1,413
Cecil	2,569	2,056	333	2,263
Charles	947	2,356	82	1,529
Dorchester	1,995	1,461	183	1,238
Frederick	3,135	3,723	1,477	3,128
Garrett	293	990	83	356
Harford	9,378	4,422	688	3,809
Howard	7,991	4,718	1,160	3,595
Kent	1,539	869	126	575
Montgomery	12,322	31,338	3,485	20,531
Prince George's	11,500	28,663	1,254	18,272
Queen Anne's	2,468	1,210	120	691
St. Mary's	1,662	3,567	277	2,707
Somerset	909	1,306	68	515
Talbot	1,936	877	78	536
Washington	2,024	5,219	577	5,234
Wicomico	2,636	2,306	239	2,134
Worcester	13,457	194,236	25,200	140,486

Table 9-5. MARYLAND CONGRESSIONAL ELECTIONS

	Democrat	Republican
	1984	
First District	Roy Dyson* 96,673	Harlan Williams 68,865
Second District	Clarence Long* 105,571	Helen Bentley 111,517
Third District	Barbara Mikulski* 113,189	Ross Pierpont 59,493
Fourth District	Howard Greenbaum 58,312	Marjorie Holt* 114,430
Fifth District	Steny Hoyer* 116,310	John Ritchie 44,838
Sixth District	Beverly Byron* 123,383	Robin Ficker 66,056
Seventh District	Parren Mitchell* 139,488	No Candidate Filed
Eighth District	Michael Barnes* 181,947	Albert Ceccone 70,715
	1982	
First District	Roy Dyson* 89,503	C. A. Porter Hopkins 39,656
Second District	Clarence Long* 83,318	Helen Bentley 75,062
Third District	Barbara Mikulski 110,042	H. Robert Sherr 38,259
Fourth District	Patricia Aiken 47,947	Marjorie Holt* 75,617
Fifth District	Steny Hoyer* 83,937	William Guthrie 21,533
Sixth District	Beverly Byron* 102,596	Roscoe Bartlett 35,321
Seventh District	Parren Mitchell* 103,496	M. Lenora Jones 14,203
Eighth District	Michael Barnes* 121,761	Elizabeth Spencer 48,910

*Indicates Incumbent

Maryland Congressional Districts

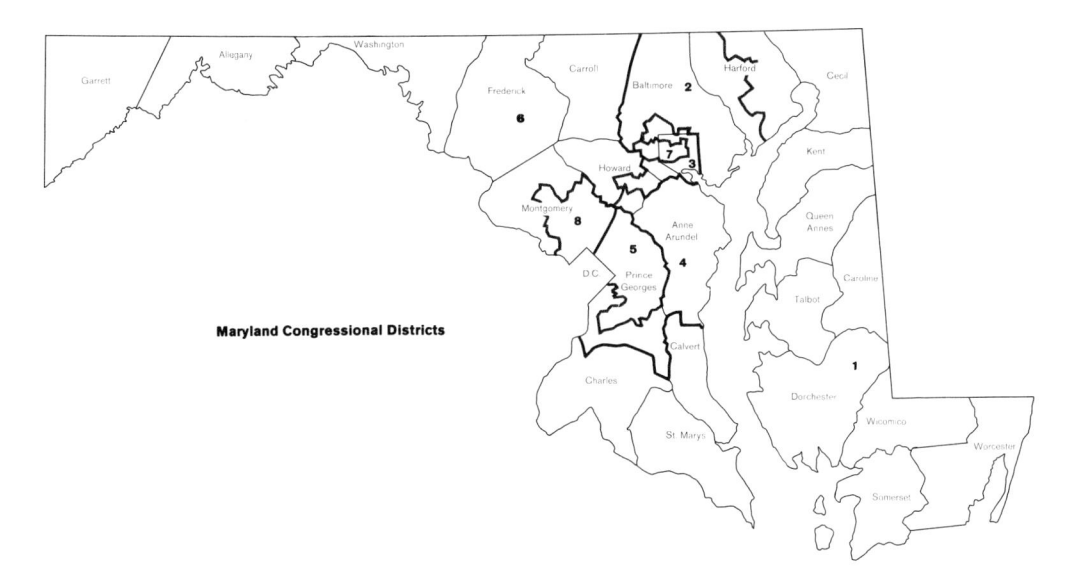

ELECTIONS WITHOUT CANDIDATES

In Maryland, at both the state and the local levels, voters have the opportunity to decide directly on some policy issues. The ballot questions include: constitutional and charter amendments, bond issues, and referendums.

Amendments to the Maryland Constitution are proposed by the General Assembly, which must approve them by a three-fifths vote of each house. The amendment is then submitted to the voters at the next General Election. Constitutional amendments may be technical and noncontroversial or they may generate widespread discussion and involve major changes in the operation of government, as in the series of amendments in the late 1960s and early 1970s that led to the reorganizations of the executive departments.

A referendum is a voter decision on a policy rather than a constitutional question. Under the Maryland Constitution, the General Assembly may provide for a referendum on local legislation that it has considered and passed. In this case, the legislation does not go into effect unless it receives voter approval. An unusual feature of this requirement is that, even though the referendum is on a local law, it requires approval by the citizens of the entire state.

There is also a referendum provision for statewide laws. If three percent of the state's voters sign a petition to bring a bill passed by the

BALLOT QUESTIONS
General Election - November 6, 1984

QUESTION NO. 1 - CONSTITUTIONAL AMENDMENT
Prohibits certain persons from entering upon the duties of, or continuing to serve in certain elective offices created by or pursuant to the Maryland Constitution if the person was not a registered voter in the State on the date of the person's election or appointment to that term or if, at anytime thereafter and prior to the completion of the term, the person ceases to be a registered voter.

QUESTION A - CHARTER AMENDMENT BY ACT OF COUNTY COUNCIL
Amend Section 305 of the County Charter to exempt the operating budgets of enterprise funds from the computation of the aggregate operating budget when making the determination as to whether the affirmative vote of five Councilmembers is required to approve the budget; to provide that the Consumer Price Index in the computation is computed for the twelve months preceding December first of each year; and to make a clarifying change.

QUESTION B - CHARTER AMENDMENT BY ACT OF COUNTY COUNCIL
Amend Section 401 of the County Charter and add Section 511 to the County Charter to authorize the County Council to provide by law for collective bargaining, with arbitration or other impasse resolution procedures, with authorized representatives of officers and employees of the County government not covered by Section 510 of the Charter; to provide that if a law is enacted it shall prohibit strikes or work stoppages for the officers and employees; and to provide that the officers and employees may be excluded from the provisions of the merit system to the extent that the provisions are subject to legislation enacted under Sections 510 or 511.

QUESTION C - CHARTER AMENDMENT BY ACT OF COUNTY COUNCIL
Amend Sections 108 and 213 of the County Charter to clarify the independent authority of the County Council to temporarily employ or retain special legal counsel to assist it in the exercise of its powers.

QUESTION D - CHARTER AMENDMENT BY REFERENDUM
Amend Section 102 of the County Charter to provide that each of five members of the Council shall no longer be nominated and elected by the voters of the entire County, but solely by the voters of the Councilmanic district in which the member resides and that the remaining two members of the Council shall be nominated and elected as members-at-large by the voters of the entire County.

QUESTION E - CHARTER AMENDMENT BY REFERENDUM
Amend Sections 102, 103 and 104 of the County Charter to divide the County into seven Councilmanic districts; to provide that each member of the Council shall no longer be nominated and elected by the voters of the entire County, but solely by the qualified voters of the Councilmanic district in which the member resides; and to provide that the boundaries of the Councilmanic districts shall be reestablished in 1986 for that year's election, in 1992, and every tenth year thereafter.

QUESTION G - REFERENDUM BY ACT OF GENERAL ASSEMBLY - 1984
To authorize the Montgomery County Board of License Commissioners to issue, renew, and transfer any class or classes of licenses for the sale of alcoholic beverages within the 2nd election district of Montgomery County.

QUESTION H - REFERENDUM BY ACT OF GENERAL ASSEMBLY - 1984
To authorize the Montgomery County Board of License Commissioners to issue, renew, and transfer any class or classes of licenses for the sale of alcoholic beverages within the 6th election district of Montgomery County.

QUESTION I - REFERENDUM BY ACT OF GENERAL ASSEMBLY - 1984
To authorize the Montgomery County Board of License Commissioners to issue, renew, and transfer any class or classes of licenses for the sale of alcoholic beverages within the 12th election district of Montgomery County.

Maryland voters have the opportunity to decide on a wide variety of ballot questions in each election.

STATEWIDE REFERENDUM
QUESTION NO. 14
Chapter 873 - 1974

AN ACT concerning Public Education - Services for Nonpublic School Children; for the purpose of providing for the loan of textbooks, instructional equipment, instructional material to nonpublic schools, and to provide for the transportation of children attending nonpublic schools in the State of Maryland, and relating generally to State aid for children attending nonpublic schools.

COUNTIES AND BALTIMORE CITY	FOR REFERRED LAW	AGAINST REFERRED LAW
Allegany	6,427	10,979
Anne Arundel	26,135	30,263
Baltimore City	59,637	49,819
Baltimore County	72,015	73,773
Calvert	1,443	2,517
Caroline	717	2,140
Carroll	4,272	7,925
Cecil	2,894	4,818
Charles	4,677	4,240
Dorchester	1,021	3,124
Frederick	4,812	8,912
Garrett	974	2,588
Harford	10,595	13,969
Howard	8,831	13,045
Kent	960	2,175
Montgomery	52,218	90,722
Prince George's	43,044	54,117
Queen Anne's	923	1,989
St. Mary's	4,007	3,048
Somerset	602	2,825
Talbot	1,770	3,086
Washington	3,554	12,259
Wicomico	2,010	9,306
Worcester	982	3,514
TOTALS	314,520	✓ 411,153

The last referendum on a statewide question was in 1974. The proposal was defeated.

In the spaces provided below, insert title of Constitutional Amendment or Legislative enactment, as it appeared upon ballot or voting machine.

1984

QUESTION NO. 1
CONSTITUTIONAL AMENDMENT

Prohibits certain persons from entering upon the duties of, or continuing to serve in certain elective offices created by or pursuant to the Maryland Constitution if the person was not a registered voter in the State on the date of the person's election or appointment to that term or if, at anytime thereafter and prior to the completion of the term, the person ceases to be a registered voter.

For ....(105,577)
Against ......(26,370)

PRINT OR TYPE THE NUMBER VOTES RECEIVED
NO PHOTOCOPY OR CARBON FIGURES

QUESTION A
PROPOSED CHARTER AMENDMENT

To include in the County real property tax limitation an alternative limitation of a maximum tax rate of $2.40 per each $100.00 of assessed valuation.

For ....(81,978)
Against ......(70,679)

PRINT OR TYPE THE NUMBER VOTES RECEIVED
NO PHOTOCOPY OR CARBON FIGURES

QUESTION B
PROPOSED CHARTER AMENDMENT

To provide for the filling of a vacancy in the Office of County Executive.

For ....(93,957)
Against ......(28,175)

PRINT OR TYPE THE NUMBER VOTES RECEIVED
NO PHOTOCOPY OR CARBON FIGURES

QUESTION C
COUNTY BUILDINGS AND FACILITIES BONDS

An Act pursuant to Section 323 of the Charter of Prince George's County, Maryland, enabling the County to borrow money and issue bonds in an amount not exceeding $2,656,000 to finance the design, construction, reconstruction, extension, acquisition, improvement, enlargement, alteration, renovation, relocation, rehabilitation or repair of County buildings and facilities, as defined therein.

For ....(78,685)
Against ......(41,119)

PRINT OR TYPE THE NUMBER VOTES RECEIVED
NO PHOTOCOPY OR CARBON FIGURES

QUESTION D
FIRE AND RESCUE FACILITIES BONDS

An Act pursuant to Section 323 of the Charter of Prince George's County, Maryland, enabling the County to borrow money and issue bonds in an amount not exceeding $338,000 to finance the design, construction, reconstruction, extension, acquisition, improvement, enlargement, alteration, renovation, relocation, rehabilitation or repair of fire and rescue facilities in the County, as defined therein.

For ....(106,000)
Against ......(20,512)

PRINT OR TYPE THE NUMBER VOTES RECEIVED
NO PHOTOCOPY OR CARBON FIGURES

The votes on some ballot questions are close while others are very one-sided.

General Assembly to referendum, that law is then voted on at the next General Election. This is, in fact, a difficult and infrequently used provision, the last example being in 1974 on a state aid to nonpublic schools law.

Local questions are much more frequent. The incurring of public debts requires voter approval in some jurisdictions. In recent years a number of controversial policy questions have also been submitted to voters in local elections. Examples include the decision on whether to build Harborplace in Baltimore City and a number of Proposition 13-type proposals limiting government spending and taxing authority.

Voter Turnout

There has been a general decline in voter turnout at elections in the United States in the last twenty to thirty years. The level varies by election—the numbers are usually highest for a presidential election and lowest for local ballot questions. The turnout is invariably higher when there are contested races, and there is the perception that the election matters. For example, the race for a party nomination in a district dominated by the opposition party is not likely to draw a large turnout. Moreover, there is always a drop-off in the number of ballots cast from the top of the ticket—the major offices—to the bottom—the constitutional amendments and ballot questions.

The evidence is clear that many citizens do not have enough interest to find out about local candidates and local questions, and end up not voting. Analysts are divided in the kinds of conclusions they reach about the effects of nonvoting.[7] Some argue that nonvoters are similar in their interests to those who vote and therefore their nonparticipation is cancelled out. The alternative position is that the people who vote and participate receive the benefits of the political system while the interests of nonparticipants may not be as well looked after. Whatever the merits of these arguments are, nonvoting remains a major characteristic of our elections.

Across the state of Maryland there has been considerable variation in voter turnout. For example, only thirty-six percent of registered Democratic and eighteen percent of registered Republicans voted in the 1984 primary election. In the General Election, the statewide proportion was over seventy-four percent, well above the national figures. Turnout in nonpresidential years is always lower and usually drops even more in strictly local elections.

Other Forms of Political Participation

One of the oldest expressions associated with local politics in America is "you can't fight City Hall." In spite of this admonition, citizens often attempt to influence the decisions of state and local governments. The means available to the public have actually increased over time. Public hearing and consultation requirements, as well as legislation which opens the way for citizens' lawsuits to compel government measures or prevent undesired actions, have all been used to make local government responsive to citizens' concerns.

There are also more traditional forms of participation. Citizens may organize in groups, either permanent or ad hoc, to try to achieve a particular result. We refer to the permanent organizations as interest groups or lobbies. While the most visible lobbying is aimed at the legislature, interest groups may attempt to influence the decision of almost any segment of government.

The First Amendment of the U. S. Constitution clearly allows and protects this activity, but individuals sometimes complain about it or describe it as inappropriate. What may be contested are the particular means employed. There are laws that regulate lobbying, including registration and financial disclosure requirements.[8]

The success of lobbying efforts is usually tied to both persistence and to skillful and informed presentation of the case. The actual influence of interest groups will vary over time and the specific issues involved. Moreover, the reputation for influence may be greater than the reality. Of two recent studies of interest groups in different states, one identified bankers, industrialists, the AFL-CIO, and the liquor lobby as strong in Maryland, while the second study listed the AFL-CIO and the Classified Employees Association.[9]

One form of political organizing that has increased dramatically in recent years is the political action committee, or PAC.[10] Changes in campaign finance laws in the 1970s have allowed committees operating independently of candidates to have great latitude in raising and spending money for political goals. The result has been that the total amount of money spent in campaigns has continued to increase sharply and the proportion of those funds provided by PACs has also increased.

The figures for Maryland parallel the national experience.[11] For example, the average PAC contribution to members of the Maryland Congressional Delegation rose from $28,432 in 1976 to $122,574 in 1984. These figures represented less than thirty percent of all campaign monies raised in 1976 and nearly fifty percent in 1984.

"And, Secondly, We Want to Avoid a Run On the STATE"

A Baltimore *Sun* cartoon on the political consequences of the savings and loan crisis.

Some observers are concerned that PACs have too much influence with elected officials because they are able to play such a key role in campaigns. One response which is offered is that PAC activity is nothing more than a legitimate form of lobbying, and that PACs tend to balance each other. In the same vein, it is sometimes argued that efforts to sharply regulate PACs will interfere with basic political freedoms.

There is no question that the level of spending on political campaigns has continued to rise, and that PAC activities have helped stimulate this increase. Whether PACs exercise excessive influence has become a central debate in our political system today. This question is as relevant to Maryland as it is to the nation as a whole.

PACs have also received attention for their independent political efforts. In a number of elections, PACs have purchased advertising and attempted to influence the outcome through their own campaigns. A notable example was the effort in 1982 of the National Conservative Political Action Committee (NCPAC) to defeat U. S. Senator Paul Sarbanes of Maryland in his reelection try. Not only was NCPAC unsuccessful, but its involvement in the campaign was seen by many political analysts as counterproductive. That experience has not, however, prevented PACs from becoming involved in other political campaigns.

Group political activity may also take the form of ad hoc coalitions which are formed in response to a specific issue and exist only long enough to engage in public discussion of that question. Recent examples in Maryland include public groups reacting to property assessment procedures and the various citizens groups established to take positions on public school financing.

Ad hoc groups sometimes maintain themselves for extended periods and many even become permanent. Citizen concern over drunk driving led to the organization of Mothers Against Drunk Driving (M.A.D.D.), which has maintained an organized effort over several legislative sessions to change the state's laws on drunk driving. Similar organizing has occurred with respect to the issue of abortion, on both sides of the question.

This kind of activity seems to contradict the generalizations about widespread apathy and nonparticipation in politics. The nature of state and local governments is such that their activities often affect people directly. An individual who may not care about the candidates running for a office may have very strong feelings about the prospect of the local elementary school being closed. While the number of people who can be described as actively involved in politics is not high, there is still evidence that more segments of the population do get involved from time to time on specific questions that affect them directly.

The Media in Politics

Most people do not participate directly in political activity. Their primary source of information about government and politics is the news media, with an increasing emphasis on television. Studies show that television has become the primary source of information for a growing proportion of people, as high as seventy percent by some accounts.[12]

The specific impact of the media on politics is hard to determine. While some observers refer to the power of the press, it is not so clear that television stations or newspapers are able to determine public policy or the winning candidates. For example, although newspapers have endorsed candidates for office for years, studies show that these endorsements are rarely critical to the outcome of elections.[13] Some observers believe an exception to this pattern may have occurred in Maryland in 1978 when the Baltimore *Sun* enthusiastically and repeatedly endorsed Harry Hughes as the Democratic nominee for governor. Hughes, considered by most political analysts to have been way behind in the race, ended up winning the nomination over two better-known candidates.

It is clear that the media, and particularly television, have become centrally involved in political campaigns. Whether or not a candidate receives coverage and is treated as a serious prospect for office is critical to the success of any campaign. Polls, often commissioned directly by the media, have become key elements in the progress of a campaign. For example, in that 1978 Democratic primary for governor, a *Sun* poll published just a few days before the election showed that Harry Hughes was only a few percentage points behind his two rivals. That information may have persuaded some voters that Hughes was a viable candidate and that they would not be wasting their vote if they supported him.

On the other hand, Benjamin Cardin, then Speaker of the House of Delegates, abandoned his campaign for the 1986 Democratic nomination for governor after numerous public polls showed him to be far behind two other candidates, William Donald Schaefer and Steve Sachs, and not getting any closer. Cardin decided in December 1985 that his low standing in the polls would prevent him from raising enough campaign funds and receiving serious attention from the press.

Candidates who are not well known and are behind in the polls are likely to use political advertising as the means to become viable candidates. This strategy is dependent on the ability to raise adequate campaign funds to pay for the ads. The enormous increase in campaign costs mentioned above is largely attributable to the high cost of ads on television.

The ability of a challenger with money to appeal to the voters through advertising forces even well-known incumbents to raise and spend large amounts of money on media advertising. In responding to NCPAC's campaign against him in 1982, Senator Paul Sarbanes spent close to a $1 million. In the 1986 election, a number of candidates raised large amounts of campaign funds with a major proportion going into media expenses.

The emphasis on the media—both attracting coverage and using advertising—is particularly evident in campaigns for statewide offices. In terms of local offices and congressional seats, the amounts of money raised and spent are usually less. Similarly, the press tends to give less attention to local races. However, there are notable exceptions. A contested mayoral race in Baltimore, as in the 1983 democratic primary, received a lot of coverage and involved heavy expenditures. A Congressional campaign, the contest between incumbent Clarence Long and challenger Helen Bentley in the Second District of Maryland in 1984, fell into the same category.

By contrast, the press may scarcely mention the candidates in many local races. Campaign expenditures total only a few thousand dollars, not enough for media advertising. In local races, ads are not an efficient means of reaching voters anyway. A television ad for a local legislative seat, for example, would be wasted on many voters who did not live in the district. More traditional campaigning, including personal appearances by the candidate, telephoning and distributing campaign literature by volunteers in addition to seeking support from organized groups, is emphasized in local elections.

The media's impact on public policy issues is a matter of some debate. Journalists tend to argue that they are merely reporting what goes on and stress their neutrality and objectivity. There are studies which conclude that the press exercises a significant amount of political power is some communities. Variations of this view are that there is evidence of systematic bias in the press, for or against particular interests or values, and that the press is able to select which events and individuals are newsworthy. Scholars refer to this as agenda-setting, that is, determining what subjects will be discussed and debated, but not necessarily what conclusions will be reached about those subjects.[14]

The press clearly affects the public policy debate when information is disclosed which people view as significant. The revelation that high level officials in the Hughes administration, including the governor, knew about problems in the state's savings and loans months before the matter became public, had an effect on public perceptions and attitudes.

Reports in the media about incidents of child abuse in schools and day care centers have helped increase public concern and awareness about this problem and have led to various changes in rules and policies.

On the other hand, the press may present information and even take editorial positions on issues without an apparent impact. The Baltimore *Sun* has strongly advocated a restructuring of the state's system of higher education over a period of several years. There has neither been any action taken on this suggestion nor any indication that there is widespread public concern about the issue.

Media in Maryland can be broken down into several different categories. There are two sets of television stations that report on government and politics in Maryland, those in Baltimore and those in Washington, D.C. A candidate running for office statewide needs to get coverage in both of those media markets and to buy advertising time in both.

On the other hand, the coverage of government and policy issues will often differ between the two markets. Washington stations are concerned with Virginia and District of Columbia news, as well as Maryland events, whereas Baltimore stations address themselves almost exclusively to the metropolitan area and the state.

In a similar way, there are two major daily newspaper markets, which have different perspectives, that parallel those of the television stations: *The Washington Post* and, in Baltimore *The Sunpapers* (the morning *Sun*, *The Evening Sun*, and the Sunday *Sun*), and until May 1986 (when it went out of business) the *News American*.

The rest of the state is served by a number of daily and weekly newspapers and several local UHF television stations. The focus of these remaining media outlets is necessarily more on local affairs than on state activity. News on state government and politics usually originates from the Baltimore and Washington, D.C. newspapers and television stations.

Conclusion

The ancient Greek concept of the complete person included active and knowledgeable participation in politics. Modern cynics have observed that people get the kind of government they deserve because they don't pay attention and stay involved in the political process.

Maryland's political history has shining examples of citizen involvement resulting in better government as well as instances of corruption and self-interested actions that ignored the public good. Neither result is guaranteed or inevitable. The choice is open to all citizens.

Chapter 10

FUTURE PROSPECTS

In the preceding chapters, we have described and examined the basic elements of government and politics at the state and local level in Maryland. The presentation in this book is only an introduction and is certainly no substitute for direct involvement in the political processes of our state. Indeed, if this book achieves its objectives, readers will be stimulated to participate directly and will be better prepared to do so.

Those who are interested and involved will help shape future developments in Maryland government. They will identify the key issues and help formulate the responses to them. While we can expect that many of the central concerns of today will continue to be important in the future, there will be new approaches to some of these issues, and developments of importance that we are not aware of now.

Any effort to identify specific issues and developments for the future would be highly speculative. It is possible, however, to discuss several factors that will affect which specific issues are important and how we deal with them in Maryland. In this chapter, four broad considerations that are likely to affect our future are examined.

MEGATRENDS

A few years ago, John Naisbitt wrote a best-seller, *Megatrends*, in which he attempted to identify major patterns of change that would affect everyone's life.[1] The idea that there are trends which are not local in origin nor subject to local control is worth considering, regardless of the specific list of factors examined. For example, national and international economic developments have a profound effect. The sharp rise in world oil prices in the 1970s affected the lives of Maryland citizens and the operation of government and business in the state in many ways. Advancing computer technology is another example of a general trend which has changed our lives in significant patterns. The increased focus on information-processing as a key economic activity is one of the major trends that Naisbitt identified in his analysis.

In the future, Maryland will clearly be affected by broad trends that are national and international in scope and origin. Those trends will help shape specific issues to which the public and the political system will need to respond.

Federalism

The relationship between the federal government and state and local governments has changed frequently over the years since the beginning of our constitutional system in 1789. We find different labels to describe federalism and refer to the most recent version as the "new federalism,"[2] a term used by Ronald Reagan in 1981 to describe his approach.

Federalism will undoubtedly continue to change. Reagan envisioned a reduction in the federal role in many programs, as well as in federal expenditures, and a shifting of responsibilities in some areas to state and local governments. Another of his objectives was to reduce government regulation of business at all levels. How much of Reagan's approach is accepted and how it will be modified are still open questions.

Efforts to reduce the federal budget deficit also relate to the nature of federalism as it is practiced. Cuts in federal assistance to state and local governments require those governments either to find alternative funding sources or to reduce or eliminate particular programs.

Different philosophies about our federal system as well as the need to make specific budget decisions will continue to affect federal, state, and local government relations in the future and to insure that those relationships will continue to change.

The consequences of these developments are of great significance for Maryland. To cite a past example, Baltimore's renaissance was certainly helped by the availability of federal funds to support key projects. Similarly, mass transit development in both Baltimore and the Washington, D.C., suburbs of Maryland was made possible by federal assistance.

A reexamination of priorities and the necessity to make new policy choices will result from any substantial reduction in the federal role. Conversely, an increase in federal activity or the initiation of new programs at that level would open up new options at the state and local levels.

State and local governments are not in the position of merely responding to actions from the federal level. Moreover, the analysis presented here is not intended to suggest that all policy choices should be national. Still, the revenue-generating capabilities of the federal government as well as the ability to develop uniform and comprehensive approaches to some issues insure that the federal role will be a central and important one in the future. Changes in the specific nature of federalism will, however, be of great significance for government at the state and local level in Maryland.

State and Local Relationships

Just as there have been changes in the nature of federalism, the state and local relationship has undergone significant adjustments. The pattern is also likely to continue to change, and the specific changes will be important to Maryland's future.

The arguments for an emphasis on either the state or the local level are familiar enough. On the one hand, the need for flexibility and the benefits of local control over local matters are very persuasive points to many citizens. The rebuttal tends to focus on the necessity of having comprehensive and uniform approaches to policy issues and on the ability of the state to match more equitably resources to needs. Neither approach has prevailed to the total exclusion of the other, but there has certainly been an expansion of the state role over the years.

Many important policy questions will be debated in terms of the relative responsibilities of state and local governments. If federal assistance drops sharply in the coming years, there is likely to be more pressure on the state to provide aid to local governments to make up for the loss of federal dollars. Programs from economic development to transportation to infrastructure needs such as water and sewer systems all fall into this category.

The nature of local government may also be subject to change in the future. As discussed in Chapter 8, regional approaches to issues may be appealing in some areas. Examples in the past have included water systems, mass transit, and solid waste disposal. Suggestions for regional approaches to such programs as education and housing have, on the other hand, met with great resistance. Whether or not opinions change on these kinds of issues will greatly influence future developments in local governments.

Political Participation

The nature and extent of citizen involvement in politics are, ultimately, the key factors that will determine the shape and direction of government in Maryland in the future. As we have pointed out, this is a familiar theme in the study of democratic governments. There are, however, some changing elements of citizen participation that merit additional comment in terms of future patterns in Maryland.

First of all, there have been some changes in the nature of political participation that are likely to be important in the future. There is significant evidence of an increased fragmentation and decentralization in the political system.[3] Political parties, one of the key unifying forces in the past, have declined greatly in their impact. Single-issue interest groups have become much more prominent and active. Mass media have become the principal sources of information about government and politics for most citizens.

These factors make the task of political leadership more difficult. One of the central tasks of any political system in the future will be to overcome fragmentation and to develop coherent policies while still preserving the democratic principles and values that we consider to be essential. The inherent tension between the procedures of democracy and the goal of effective government will have a major impact on the issues we face in the future and on the ways in which we respond to them.

A second major factor is that the relationship between government and the private sector has continued to change.[4] The concept of public-private partnerships has become increasingly important in many areas. Government has become very active as a promoter of economic development activities, and private institutions have become more involved in programs and services that, until fairly recently, were considered purely public.

The movement toward "privatization" of certain public services is illustrated in the private firms that operate prisons in some areas under contract with the responsible governmental unit. Another example of the changing public-private relationship is the development of organizations that are quasi-public, that is, affiliated with government, but operating more like private institutions. Baltimore has used this approach extensively in its economic development efforts.

The effect of these developments is that government is no longer the only participant in public policy decision making. In one sense, this change reinforces the fragmentation of the political system that was just discussed. On the other hand, it opens up the political system to more viewpoints and more participants. The need for collaboration and cooperation, which is a requirement of our system of divided powers and institutions, may be met by the opportunities for participation that these changes seem to provide.

The effectiveness and success of government in Maryland at both the state and the local levels are matters of great importance. These concerns are not isolated from the health and vitality of the community as a whole, but are, rather, a central part of it. Government is one of the primary means by which a society deals with the issues and problems that confront it. How well the governing process is carried out affects all aspects of life. The interest and effort which we as citizens put into that undertaking will determine the kind of future that we have.

NOTES

Chapter 1. Introduction

1. *Power in the States: The Changing Face of Politics Across America* (Washington, D.C.: Congressional Quarterly, Inc., 1984), p. 44
2. See the collection of essays in Herrington J. Bryce, ed., *Urban Governance and Minorities* (New York: Praeger, 1976).
3. See, for example, President's Commission on Industrial Competitiveness, *Global Competition: The New Reality* (Washington, D.C.: Government Printing Office, 1985).
4. Donald Marquand Dozer, *Portrait of the Free State: A History of Maryland* (Centreville, Md.: Tidewater Publishers, 1976), p. 1.
5. George H. Callcott, *Maryland and America 1940 to 1980* (Baltimore: Johns Hopkins University Press, 1985), Ch. 1.
6. See William Warner, *Beautiful Swimmers: Watermen, Crabs, and the Chesapeake Bay* (Boston: Little, Brown, 1976).
7. For a discussion of the concept of "positive" government, see Kenneth J. Meier, *Politics and the Bureaucracy* (Boston: Duxbury Press, 1979), Ch. 1.
8. See Morton Grodzins, *The American System* (Chicago: Rand, McNally, 1974).

Chapter 2. The Constitutional System of Maryland

1. A sampling of studies on federalism include: Daniel Elasar, *American Federalism: A View from the States* (New York: Crowell, 1984); Parris Glendening and Mavis Reeves, *Pragmatic Federalism* (Palisades, Calif.: Palisades Publishers, 1984); and David Walker, *Toward a Functioning*

Federalism (Cambridge, Mass.: Winthrop, 1981).
2. United States Department of Commerce, Bureau of the Census. *Statistical Abstract of the United States* (Washington, D.C.: Government Printing Office, 1985).
3. These arguments are examined in Advisory Commission on Intergovernmental Relations, *The Question of State Government Capability* (Washington, D. C.: GPO, 1985), Ch. 1.
4. Ibid., Ch. 3. A review of state constitutional activity as well as of information sources can be found in the biennially published *The Book of the States* (Lexington, Ky: Council of State Governments).
5. See Richard Nathan and Fred Doolittle, *The Consequences of Cuts: The Effects of the Reagan Domestic Program on State and Local Governments* (Princeton Urban and Regional Research Center, 1983). The continuing nature of this issue is shown in Robert Rothman, "Cities, States Say Cuts in Aid will Create an Unfair Burden," *Congressional Quarterly*, 43 (February 16, 1985).
6. For a general discussion of this issue, see, for example, Richard Cortner, *The Apportionment Case* (Knoxville: University of Tennessee Press, 1970); and Nelson Polsby, ed., *Reapportionment in the 1970's* (Berkeley: University of California Press, 1971).
7. These events are described in John Wheeler and Melissa Kinsey, *Magnificent Failure: The Maryland Constitutional Conversion of 1967-1968* (National Municipal League, 1970).
8. Whether or not the Bill of Rights applies, or is "incorporated," in the states is discussed by Henry Abraham, *Freedom and the Courts* (New York: Oxford University Press, 1982).
9. Key decisions include: *Guinn v. United States, 238 U.S. 347 (1915); Newberry v. United States*, 256 U.S. 232 (1927); *Smith v. Allwright*, 321 U.S. 649 (1944); *Harper v. Virginia State Board of Elections*, 383 U.S. 663 (1966). A major step was taken in 1965 when the Federal Voting Rights Act was passed. See the discussion in Henry Abraham, *Freedom and the Courts* (New York: Oxford University Press, 1982).
10. An examination of judicial elections in different states is presented in Mary Volcansek, "An Exploration of the Judicial Election Process," *The Western Political Quarterly*, 34, no. 4 (December 1981). See also, Susan Carbon, "Judicial Retention Elections: Are They Serving Their Intended Purpose," *Judicature*, 64 (1980).
11. *Somerset County Board of Education v. Hornbeck*, 458 A2d. 758 (1983).

Chapter 3. The Governor

1. Charles James Rohr, *The Governor of Maryland: A Constitutional Study* (Baltimore: Johns Hopkins University Press, 1932), p. 5.

2. Two recent studies on the powers of governors are: Larry Sabato, *Goodbye To Good Time Charlie* (Washington, D.C.: Congressional Quarterly, Inc., 1983); and Thad Beyle and Lynn Muchmore, eds., *Being Governor: The View from the Office* (Durham, N.C.: Duke University Press, 1983). Research on mayors often stresses the limitations on power, as in Douglas Yates, *The Ungovernable City* (Cambridge, Mass.: MIT Press, 1977). Examples of effective mayoral leadership are discussed in, for example, Martha Wagner Weinberg, "Boston's Kevin White: A Mayor Who Survives," *Political Science Quarterly*, 96, no. 1 (Spring 1981); and various works on Richard Daley of Chicago, such as Mike Royko, *Boss* (New York: Signet, 1971).
3. A good discussion of public expectations about the presidency can be found in Thomas Cronin, *The State of the Presidency* (Boston: Little, Brown and Company, 1980). For a look at governors, see, Parris N. Glendening, "The Public's Perception of State Government and Governors," *State Government* (Summer 1980).
4. For an account of this period, see Bradford Jacobs, *Thimbleriggers: The Law v. Marvin Mandel* (Baltimore: Johns Hopkins University Press, 1984).
5. The powers of governors of different states are evaluated in Thad Beyle, "Governors," in Virginia Gray, Herbert Jacob, and Kenneth Vines, eds., *Politics in the American States* (Boston: Little, Brown and Company, 1983). Another approach to the same topic is Nelson Dometrius, "Measuring Gubernatorial Power," *Journal of Politics*, 41 (1979).
6. For a discussion of the Board of Public Works, see Tom Linthicum, "State Panel: The Power and the Trivia," Baltimore *Sun*, December 18, 1983.
7. The key work is Richard Neustadt, *Presidential Power* (New York: John Wiley and Sons, Inc., 1980). Neustadt's analysis has influenced most other students of executive leadership. See also, E. Lee Bernick, "Gubernatorial Tools: Formal vs. Informal." *The Journal of Politics*, 41 (1979).
8. Neustadt, *Presidential Power*.
9. See, for example, Beyle, "Governors."
10. This point is discussed by Sabato, Glendening, and Beyle, among others.
11. Sabato examines career patterns available to governors. See *Goodbye to Good Time Charlie*, Chs. 2 and 6.

Chapter 4. The State Legislature of Maryland

1. Quoted in Ann Elder and George Kiser, *Governing American States and Communities* (Glenview, Ill.: Scott, Foresman and Company, 1983), p. 126.
2. See Alan Rosenthal, *Legislative Life: People, Process and Performance in the States* (New York: Harper and Row, 1981), for a discussion of recent changes.

3. These dual functions are considered by William Keefe and Morris Ogul, *The American Legislative Process: Congress and the States* (Englewood Cliffs, N.J.: Prentice Hall, 1985); Rosenthal, *Legislative Life*; and others.
4. A thoughtful examination of this point can be found in Lester Thurow, *The Zero-Sum Society* (New York: Basic Books, 1980).
5. *Baker* v. *Carr*, 369 US. 186 (1962). For a review of this issue, see Richard Cortner, *The Apportionment Cases* (Knoxville, Tenn.: University of Tennessee Press, 1970).
6. See, for example, James David Barber, *The Lawmakers: Recruitment and Adaptation to Legislative Life* (New Haven, Conn.: Yale University Press, 1965).
7. See Rosenthal, *Legislative Life*, Ch. 8.
8. An excellent analysis of the role of committees is contained in Richard Fenno, *Congressmen in Committees* (Boston: Little, Brown and Company, 1973). Keefe and Ogul discuss this topic in Chs. 6-7.
9. For a good overview of the importance of rules and procedures in legislatures, see Walter Oleszek, *Congressional Procedures and The Policy Process* (Washington, D.C.: Congressional Quarterly Inc., 1984).
10. See the discussion of this interpretation in *Legislator's Handbook* (The Maryland General Assembly, 1982), p. 41.
11. Newspaper coverage of the Maryland General Assembly often focuses on the activities of lobbyists. See, for example, C. Fraser Smith, "Legislators Have Their Pick of Receptions, Gifts During Session," Baltimore *Sun*, January 28, 1985; and a series by C. Fraser Smith on political fundraising, Baltimore *Sun*, February 23, 1986-February 27, 1986.

Chapter 5. The Courts and the Judicial System

1. The Supreme Court decision in *U.S.* v. *Nixon*, 418 U.S. 683 (1974), was a key factor in the eventual resignation of President Nixon.
2. See Chapter 2, note 6, for citations on reapportionment.
3. See William L. Reynolds II, "The Court of Appeals of Maryland: Roles, Work and Performance," 37 *Maryland Law Review*, (1977); and Reynolds, "The Court of Appeals of Maryland: Roles, Work and Performance. Part II: Craftsmanship and Decision-Making," 38 *Maryland Law Review* 2 (1978).
4. *Kelly* v. *R. G. Industries, Inc.* 497 A2d 1143 (1985).
5. *Gideon* v. *Wainwright*, 372 U.S. 335 (1963). For a discussion of this case, see Anthony Lewis, *Gideon's Trumpet* (New York: Random House, 1964).
6. See Alexander Bickel, *The Least Dangerous Branch* (Indianapolis, Ind.: Bobbs-Merrill, 1962).
7. The point is discussed by Herbert Jacob, *Justice in America: Courts, Lawyers, and the Judicial Process* (Boston: Little, Brown, 1984).

NOTES 185

8. See J. Anthony Lukas, *Common Ground* (New York: Alfred A. Knopf, 1985).
9. Henry Abraham examines this controversy in *Freedom and the Courts* (New York: Oxford University Press, 1982).

Chapter 6. The Administration of State Government: Bureaucrats and Bureaucracy

1. A good review of recent criticism of bureaucracy is Herbert Kaufman, "Fear of Bureaucracy: A Raging Pandemic," *Public Administration Review* 41, no. 1 (Jan/Feb 1981). See also, Kenneth J. Meier, *Politics and the Bureaucracy* (Boston: Duxbury Press, 1979), Ch. 1.
2. See Charles Goodsell, *The Case for Bureaucracy* (Chatham, N.J.: Chatham House, 1983).
3. U. S. Department of Commerce, Bureau of the Census, *Public Employment in 1983* (Washington, D.C.: Government Printing Office, 1984).
4. Maryland Department of Personnel, *Annual Report* (1984).
5. The history of the merit system is reviewed in O. Glenn Stahl, *Public Personnel Administration* (New York: Harper and Row, 1983), Ch. 2. See also Dennis Dresang, *Public Personnel Management and Policy* (Boston: Little, Brown, 1984), Ch. 2.
6. See, for example, David Stanley, "What are Unions Doing to Merit Systems?" *Public Personnel Review*, 25 (April 1970). Also, Douglas McIntyre, "Merit Principles and Collective Bargaining: A Marriage or a Divorce," *Public Administration Review*, (Mar/Apr 1977).
7. The most recent is the *1983 Report of the Task Force to Study the Funding of Public Educaton* (Annapolis, 1983), better known as the Civiletti Commission Report.
8. For a good discussion of the concept of redistributive policy, see Randall Ripley and Grace Franklin, *Congress, the Bureaucracy, and Public Policy* (Homewood, Ill.: Dorsey Press, 1984).

Chapter 7. Local Government in Maryland

1. For an examination of the role of community groups in the political process that draws upon research in Baltimore, see Matthew Crenson, *Neighborhood Politics* (New York: Oxford University Press, 1983).
2. Russell Hanson, "The Intergovernmental Setting of State Politics," in Virginia Gray, Herbert Jacob, and Kenneth Vines, *Politics in the American States* (Boston: Little, Brown, 1983), 41.
3. John F. Dillon, *Commentaries on the Law of Municipal Corporations* (Boston: Little, Brown, 1911), vol. I, sec. 237.
4. U. S. Department of Commerce, Bureau of the Census, *1982 Census of*

Governments (Washington, D.C.: Government Printing Office, 1983).
5. The distinction between independent and dependent school districts is examined in Marilyn Gittell, *Six Urban School Districts* (New York: Praeger, 1968).
6. The standard reference for special districts is still John Bollens, *Special District Government in the United States* (Berkeley: University of California Press, 1957). See the discussion in Robert Lorch, *State and Local Government* (Englewood Cliffs, N.J.: Prentice-Hall, Inc., 1983), 275-80.
7. See M. Peter Moser, "County Home Rule—Sharing the State's Legislative Power with Maryland Counties, 28 *Maryland Law Review* 4 (Fall 1968).
8. *Mayor and City Council of Baltimore* v. *Crockett*, 415 A2d 606 (1980).
9. See, for example, the discussion of interdependence in metropolitan areas in Ann Elder and George Kiser, *Governing American States and Communities* (Glenview, Ill.: Scott, Foresman and Company, 1983), Ch. 14.
10. For a review of the efforts at regional cooperation, see John J. Harrigan, *Political Change in the Metropolis* (Boston: Little, Brown, 1985), Ch. 11.

Chapter 8. Baltimore City

1. Neal R. Peirce and Jerry Hagstrom, *The Book of America: Inside 50 States Today* (New York: W. W. Norton, Co., 1983), p. 132.
2. The list of studies is a long one. See, for example, Edward Banfield, *The Unheavenly City Revisited* (Boston: Little, Brown, 1974); Robert Lineberry and Ira Sharkansky, *Urban Politics and Public Policy* (New York: Harper and Row, 1978); and Douglas Yates, *The Ungovernable City* (Cambridge, Mass.: MIT Press, 1977).
3. Michael Harrington, *The Other America: Poverty in the United States* (New York: Macmillan, 1962).
4. Joel Aberback and Jack Walker, *Race in the City* (Boston: Little, Brown, 1973).
5. See Banfield, *The Unheavenly City*.
6. Yates, *The Ungovernable City*.
7. This concept has been used in school finance suits. See the discussion by Erick Lindman, *Dilemmas of School Finance* (Arlington, Va.: Educational Research Service, Inc., 1975).
8. Donald Baker, "Is Baltimore Truly Back?", *Washington Post*, November 24, 1984.
9. For two recent works, see Suzanne Greene, *Baltimore: An Illustrated History* (Brightwaters, N.Y.: Windsor, 1980); and Sherry Olson, *Baltimore: The Building of an American City* (Baltimore: Johns Hopkins University Press, 1980).
10. See Jeffrey Pressman, "Preconditions of Maryland Leadership," *American Political Science Review*, 66, no. 2 (June 1972).

11. This section is based upon an analysis in Laslo Boyd, "Mayoral Leadership: William Donald Schaefer and the Revitalization of Baltimore," a paper presented at the Annual Meeting of the Northeast Political Science Association, Boston, November 15–17, 1984.
12. The trustees system has received a lot of attention, both local and national. See the July 1980 series in the Baltimore *Sun*. Also, the United States Conference of Mayors, *The Baltimore City Loan and Guarantee Program: A Trustee System* (April 1984). In March 1986, the Schaefer Administration announced that the Loan and Guarantee Program would be dismantled.
13. To cite just two examples, see Neal Peirce, "Dazzling Baltimore," Baltimore *Sun*, June 30, 1980; and Richard Ben Cramer, "Can the Best Mayor Win?" *Esquire* (October 1984).
14. For an analysis of the economics of cities, see James Heilbrun, *Urban Economics and Public Policy* (New York: St. Martin's, 1981).
15. This issue is discussed in Regional Planning Council, *General Development Plan, 1986* (Baltimore, Maryland). The Regional Planning Council's report contains a number of dramatic proposals for regional cooperation.

Chapter 9. Politics and Elections

1. For a recent discussion of political participation, see, for example, Margaret Conway, *Political Participation in the United States* (Washington, D.C.: Congressional Quarterly, Inc., 1985). Also, Everett Carl Ladd, *Where Have All the Voters Gone?* (New York: W. W. Norton, & Co., 1982); and Sidney Verba and Norman Nie, *Participation in America* (New York: Harper and Row, 1972).
2. See Gabriel Almond and Sidney Verba, *The Civic Culture* (Princeton, N.J.: Princeton University Press, 1963), and Daniel Elazar, *American Federalism: A View from the States* (New York: Crowell, 1984).
3. A thoughtful examination of this topic is Raymond Wolfinger and Steven Rosenstone, *Who Votes?* (New Haven, Conn.: Yale University Press, 1980).
4. This argument is examined in William Crotty, *American Parties in Decline* (Boston: Little, Brown, 1984).
5. See Larry Sabato, *The Rise of Political Consultants* (New York: Basic Books, 1982). Also, Robert Agranoff, *The Management of Election Campaigns* (Oxford, Mass.: Holbrook Press, 1976).
6. Studies on voting behavior are numerous. For a good review, see William Flanigan and Nancy Zingale, *Political Behavior of the American Electorate* (Newton, Mass.: Allyn and Bacon, 1983).
7. In addition to the previous references on voting studies, see Arthur Hadley, *The Empty Polling Booth* (Englewood Cliffs, N.J.: Prentice-Hall, 1978);

and Norman Nie, Sidney Verba, and John Petrocik, *The Changing American Voter* (Boston: Harvard University Press, 1976).
8. The Maryland Public Ethics Law is contained in Article 40A of the Maryland Annotated Code. The State Ethics Commission has published a summary pamphlet, *Maryland Public Ethics Law Summary*.
9. See L. Harmon Zeigler, "Interest Groups in the States," in Virginia Gray, Herbert Jacob and Kenneth Vines, eds., *Politics in the American States* (Boston: Little, Brown, 1983), p. 102, and Michael Engel, *State and Local Politics* (New York: St. Martin's Press, 1985), p. 241.
10. See Larry Sabato, *PAC Power: Inside the World of Political Action Committees* (New York: W. W. Norton & Co., 1984).
11. See Edward Roeder, "PACs Play Major Role in Maryland," Sunday *Sun*, August 25, 1985.
12. See the discussion in Doris Graber, *Mass Media and American Politics* (Washington, D.C.: Congressional Quarterly, Inc., 1984).
13. See H. A. Scarrow and S. Borman, "Effects of Newspaper Endorsements on Election Outcomes: A Case Study," *Public Opinion Quarterly*, 43 (Fall 1979).
14. See for example, Donald Shaw and Maxwell McCombs, *The Emergence of American Political Issues: The Agenda-Setting Function of the Press* (St. Paul, Minn.: West Publishing Company, 1977).

Chapter 10. Future Prospects

1. John Naisbitt, *Megatrends* (New York: Warner Books, Inc., 1982).
2. See the references on federalism listed in Chapter 2, note 1.
3. This perspective is discussed in Anthony King, "The American Polity in the Late 1970's: Building Coalitions in the Sand," in Anthony King, ed., *The New American Political System* (Washington, D.C.: American Enterprise Institute, 1978). For a thoughtful presentation of the same point at the local level, see Douglas Yates, *The Ungovernable City* (Cambridge, Mass.: MIT Press, 1978).
4. Among recent studies are E. S. Savas, *Privatizing the Public Sector* (Chatham, N.J.: Chatham House, 1982) and Annmarie Hauck Walsh, *The Public's Business: The Politics and Practices of Government Corporations* (Cambridge, Mass.: MIT Press, 1978).

SUGGESTED READINGS

For those seeking further information, a variety of resources is available. The State of Maryland issues a number of useful publications about its activities. The two key volumes, published annually, are the *Maryland Manual* (Maryland State Archives) and the *Maryland Statistical Abstract* (Department of Economic and Community Development). In addition, other state departments and agencies publish both annual reports and statistical information about a wide range of programs and problems. Commissions and task forces also issue findings and conclusions.

The two legislative support agencies, the Department of Fiscal Services and the Department of Legislative Reference, are both excellent sources of information.

A number of national organizations publish comparative materials about the states. One particularly good general source is *The Book of the States*, published biannually by the Council of State Governments, Lexington, Kentucky. Materials on the states are also available from the National Governors' Association, the National Association of State Legislatures, the Advisory Commission on Intergovernmental Relations, and the Census Bureau of the U. S. Department of Commerce.

Information about specific topics appears in the news media and is also available from a number of other sources. Legal and constitutional issues, for example, are examined in the law reviews published by the University of Baltimore and the University of Maryland. Professional associations and other organizations often prepare written materials about issues that concern them that are being considered by the General Assembly.

INDEX

Administrative, Executive, and Legislative Review Committee, 68
Administrative Office of the Courts, 90
AFL-CIO, 170
Agnew, Spiro T., 43
Agriculture, Department of, 106, 108, 113
Allegany County, 118, 124
"America in Miniature," 15
American Federation of State, County, and Municipal Employees (AFSCME), 101
Anne Arundel County, 121
Appropriations, Committee on, 66

Baker v. *Carr*, 33
Baltimore City, 18, 33, 47, 116, 118, 121, 124, 125, 137-54
  business and industry, 143-44
  characteristics, 142-44
  Council, 144-45
  economy, 13
  form of government, 144-50
  government and economic development, 150-79
  history, 141-44
  population, 10, 21
  renaissance, 150-52
  "strong mayor" system, 145-46
  "two Baltimores," 152
Baltimore County, 121
Bentley, Helen, 174
Boards, advisory, 110
Bond issues, 165
Budget and Audit, Joint Committee on, 68
―――― and Fiscal Planning, Department of, 45, 104
―――― and Taxation Committee, 64
Bureaucracy
  characteristics, 98

  criticism, 97
  Maryland, 110-13
  merit system, 98
  unionization, 100-1

Cabinet
  departments, 103, 106, 108-10
  functions, 102, 104
  secretaries, 102, 104
Callcott, George, 18, 21
Cardin, Benjamin, 173
Carroll County, 118
Charles County, 118
Chesapeake Bay, 18, 24, 50, 54, 120, 131
Circuit Court, Maryland, 83
Civiletti Commission, 112
Classified Employees Association, 170
Collective bargaining, 101
Commissions, 110
Committees, House of Delegates, 64, 66
――――, Senate, 66-67
Conference Committee, 68
Constitutional Convention of 1967, 36
Constitution and Administrative Law, Committee on, 66
Constitution of Maryland, 87, 111, 120-24, 155
  amendments, 33, 34, 73, 165
  constitutional convention, 33, 34
  Declaration of Rights, 43, 77
  governor, 36, 43-47
  judiciary, 36
  legislature, 36, 73
  voting, 44
Cooperative federalism, 30
County commissioner system, 122, 124
County government, 116
Court of Appeals, Maryland, 83
Court of Special Appeals, Maryland, 83-85, 86

INDEX

Court system, Maryland
  Caseload, 80-89
  Circuit Court, 85
  Court of Appeals, 86-91
  Court of Special Appeals, 83-85, 86
  District Court, 79-83
  Jurisdiction, 79-80, 83-85, 86-87
Critical Areas Commission, 120
Cumberland, Maryland, 13

Declaration of Rights, 33, 73
Democratic party, 156-57
Demographics, 10-15, 21-22
Dillon's Rule, 114, 122
District Court, Maryland, 79-83
Dual federalism, 30

Economic and Community Development, Department of, 108
Economic and Environmental Affairs Committee, 64
Economic Matters, Committee on, 67
Economy, 12-14
Education, 11, 37, 50, 52, 74, 79, 89, 111, 120, 125, 175
———, Higher, State Board of, 110
———, State Department of, 109-10
Elections, Maryland, 157-60
  one-party state, 156-57
  primaries, 157
  split tickets, 156
  voter turnout, 169
Employment and Training, Department of, 108
Environmental Matters, Committee on, 67
Ethics Commission, State, 75
Executive budget, 45, 73
Executive leadership, 39-40
Express Powers Act, 122

Federal government, growth of, 24, 30
Federalism, 24, 26, 28, 37, 102, 111, 154, 177-78
  cooperative, 30
  dual, 30
  new, 30, 177
Federal Relations, Joint Committee on, 68
Finance Committee, 66
Fiscal Services, Department of, 68

Garrett County, 10
Garrity, Arthur, 94
General Services, Department of, 104
Gideon v. *Wainwright*, 94
Government, 98, 100-2
Governor
  budget message, 73
  characteristics, 41
  executive budget, 73
  formal powers, 43-47
  informal powers, 48-50

  qualifications, 41
  roles: chief executive, 51-52; initiator, 49-50; intermediary, 54; policy maker, 52-54; political, 54-55
  staff, 48-49
Governor's Salary Commission, 36, 43
Grants, 127-29
Greenbag, 44

Hagerstown, Maryland, 13
Hanson, John, 23
Harford County, 121
Health and Mental Hygiene, Department of, 102, 108, 112
Home rule, 37-38
  Maryland constitutional provisions: Article XI-A, 121-22; Article XI-E, 122; Article XI-F, 118; county commissioner system, 122, 124; Express Powers Act, 122
House Protocol Committee, 67
Howard County, 11, 13, 118, 121
Hughes, Harry, 41, 47, 54, 160, 174

Income tax, 126
Independent agencies, 110
Intergovernmental transfer payments, 127-28
Interstate agencies, 110

Joint committees, 67-68
Journalists, 173-75
Judges, selection of, 91-92, 93
Judicial Proceedings Committee, 66
Judiciary. *See* Courts
Judiciary, Committee on the, 67

Kaplan, Joseph, 94
Kelly v. *R. G. Industries*, 89
Kent County, 10, 118, 122, 125
Key, Francis Scott, 23

Law Examiners, State Board of, 90
Lee, Blair, 43, 160
Legislative Council, 67-68
Legislative Ethics Committee, 68
Legislative Policy Committee, 64, 67-68
Legislative Reference, Department of, 68, 69
Legislator
  characteristics, 61-63
  dual role, 57, 77
Legislature
  characteristics, 61-63
  committees, 64, 66-68
  conference committee, 68
  elections, 58, 59, 61
  history, 23, 57
  joint committees, 67-68
  leadership, 62, 64
  organization, 62, 64, 66-68
  powers, 73-77

procedures, 71-79
process, 68-71
Licensing and Regulation, Department of, 109
Lieutenant governor, office of, 43, 44
Lobbyists, 75-77
Local control, 19-20, 114, 120, 133-34, 139-40, 178
Local government
 budgets, 125-31
 expenditures, 125-26
 forms of: county, 116; municipality, 116; powers, 114-15, 120-24; resources, 126-27; school district, 118; special district, 118
 revenues, 126-27
Long, Clarence, 174

MADD, 172
Management of Public Funds, Joint Committee on, 68
Mandel, Marvin, 43
Maryland and America 1940 to 1980, 18, 21
Maryland Classified Employees Association (MCEA), 100-1
Maryland Committee v. *Tawes*, 33
Maryland Legal Services Corporation, 94
Mathias, Charles, 160
Media, role of, 9, 40, 50, 78, 97, 172-75
Megatrends, 176-77
Merit system, 98, 100, 102
Montgomery County, 118, 121
Municipalities, 116
"Municipal overburden," 140

Naisbitt, John, 176
National Governors' Association, 51, 54
Natural Resources, Department of, 102, 108
NCPAC, 172
New federalism, 30, 177

Ocean City, Maryland, 18
One-party state, 156-57

Personnel, Department of, 83, 100, 104-6
Political Action Committees (PACs), 170-72
Political culture, 155
Planning, Department of State, 106, 113
Primaries, 157
Prince Georges County, 118, 121
Privatization, 179
Property tax, 126
Public Defender, Office of the, 93-94
Public employee unions, 100-1
Public-private partnerships, 179
Public Safety and Correctional Services, Department of, 108-9
Public Works, Board of, 47

Race relations, 11, 139
Reapportionment, 33, 61, 78
 Baker v. *Carr*, 33
 Maryland Committee v. *Tawes*, 33
Referendum, 165, 169
Regional cooperation, 133-34, 153, 178-79
Regulations, government, 26, 30, 177
Representation, theory of, 27
Republican party, 157
Rockville, Maryland, 118, 137
Rules and Executive Nominations, Committee on, 67

Sachs, Steve, 173
St. Mary's County, 10
Salisbury, Maryland, 13
Sarbanes, Paul, 160, 172, 173
Schaefer, William Donald, 42, 146, 152, 160, 173
School districts, 118
Senate President, 64, 67, 74
Separation of powers, 56
Somerset County, et al v. *Hornbeck*, 37
Speaker of the House, 64, 67, 74
Special districts, 118
Spending Affordability, Joint Committee on, 68
Split tickets, 156
State's Attorney, Office of the, 93

Talbot County, 10, 121
Taney, Roger, 23
Task forces, 110
Transportation, Department of, 109, 113

U. S. Constitution, 28, 30, 61, 73, 90-91, 93-94, 114, 155, 170
U. S. Supreme Court, 61
Urban crisis, 138
Urban government, 139
Urban problems
 infrastructure, 139, 140
 population, 138
 poverty, 138
 race and class, 139

Venetoulis, Ted, 160
Veterans, 45, 47, 70-71
Voter turnout, 169

Washington, D. C., 18
Washington County, 118
Ways and Means, Committee on, 67
Wealth, 11-12
Wicomico County, 121
Worcester County, 118

Yates, Douglas, 139

CIRCULATION COLLECTION
GERMANTOWN

MONTGOMERY COLLEGE LIBRARIES
0 0000 00405221 3